The A–Z
of
SUCCESS

BY

ANDY HOLLIGAN

Shield Crest

ISBN: 978-1-911090-85-4
First Edition
Second Edition

A CIP catalogue record for this book
is available from the British Library

MMXVIII

Published by

ShieldCrest
Aylesbury, Buckinghamshire, HP18 0TF
England.

www.shieldcrest.co.uk

To my niece Abbie Jamieson
and my nephew Nicholas Carr,
with love.

CONTENTS

for ATTITUDE

If you were to carry out a survey consisting entirely of extremely successful people and ask them what they thought were the most important attributes required for success, you would probably find that a positive mental attitude was either number one on their list or very close to it. Your attitude will determine how far you go in life and is the one thing over which you have absolute control. It cannot be stolen or given away without your permission, and it determines your level of happiness. Although some people or situations may threaten to steal or destroy your attitude, ultimately we make the decision of whether our attitude will be positive or negative.

The first step in developing a positive mental attitude is to take responsibility. We must realise that we alone are responsible for our attitude. Once we have accepted that, then we can start to work on developing a positive mental attitude. But what exactly is a positive mental attitude? The dictionary defines it as "a mental position with regard to a fact." Other definitions include "outlook, view, disposition, demeanour, and perspective." Our attitude is the lens through which we view our life and our experiences. It colours and taints everything we look at. The more positive our attitude, the more we are able to rise above everyday challenges that threaten to overwhelm us. If we find ourselves having a negative attitude because of a particular event or situation, we must realise that it's not the event or situation that has caused us to feel that way, but ourselves. We have chosen to react that way. For example, what is your attitude when the following situations occur?

- THE WEATHER IS BAD
- SOMEONE CUTS YOU OFF IN TRAFFIC
- SOMEONE COMPLAINS ABOUT YOUR PRODUCT OR SERVICE
- THINGS DON'T WORK OUT AS PLANNED
- YOU FAIL AT SOMETHING
- SOMEONE LETS YOU DOWN FOR A BUSINESS APPOINTMENT
- SOMETHING YOU WERE LOOKING FORWARD TO IS CANCELLED
- YOU HAVE TO WAIT IN LINE
- A BUSINESS PROJECT THAT YOU'RE WORKING ON IS EXPERIENCING SETBACK AFTER SETBACK
- YOU SPEAK TO SOMEONE AND THEY IGNORE YOU

These are just a few examples of many potential situations that occur in everyday life. But the important thing is not what happens to us, but how we respond. How we respond is always a choice. We must be careful not to let negative emotions control our responses, and respond positively instead. For example, if you had to wait in line, instead of responding with anger why not respond with patience instead? A lot of how we respond has to do with the internal dialogues we have with ourselves at those particular moments. We start telling ourselves negative things, and this results in causing negative emotions. We need to control what we tell ourselves, and then we will control our emotions.

Many things happen to us that we either have little or no control over, but our attitude is the one thing that we do have total control over. Ask yourself, based on each example, which would most likely be your response:

1. The weather is bad and you were planning an outdoor activity with some friends.
    DO YOU: moan and complain about how miserable the weather is?
    OR DO YOU: quickly devise a "plan B" and go somewhere else which is indoors instead?

2. Someone cuts you off in traffic.
    DO YOU: get angry and honk the horn?
    OR DO YOU: rise above it and stay calm?

3. Someone complains about your product or service.
    DO YOU: immediately get defensive and give them a piece of your mind?
    OR DO YOU: consider whether the complaint is justified or not, and try to see their point of view before responding?

4. Things don't work out as planned.
    DO YOU: get angry and become pessimistic, possibly using negative words?
    OR DO YOU: adjust your schedule according to the changing events and make the best out of a bad situation?

5. You fail at something.
    DO YOU: give up and tell yourself that you're hopeless at that, and it wasn't meant to be?
    OR DO YOU: keep trying, no matter how long it takes

to succeed, and tell yourself that you'll do whatever it takes?

6. Someone lets you down for a business appointment.
   DO YOU: get angry and start thinking negative thoughts about them?
   OR DO YOU: tell yourself, "They obviously weren't the right person," and use your time and energy to find someone else?

7. Something you were looking forward to is cancelled.
   DO YOU: become pessimistic, and go on and on about it, telling every person you meet?
   OR DO YOU: handle your disappointment by focusing on what you've got going for you, realising that there are millions of people in this world who would love to change places with you?

8. You have to wait in line.
   DO YOU: get angry and start complaining?
   OR DO YOU: accept the fact that you sometimes have to wait, and use that time to strike up a conversation?

9. A business project you are working on is experiencing setback after setback.
   DO YOU: lose heart and decide to give up and do something else?
   OR DO YOU: accept that nothing worthwhile comes easy and realise that this is just part of the process of becoming successful?

10. You speak to someone and they ignore you.
    DO YOU: assume the worst and think that they either don't like you or that you've done something wrong?
    OR DO YOU: think, "So what? maybe they were deep in thought or there's some other valid reason?"

Our attitude probably affects more areas of our lives than we would like to admit. Although attitude isn't the only thing, it is certainly the foundation for everything else. A person with a positive mental attitude and little education will go a lot further in life than someone who is highly educated but has a negative attitude. Thomas Edison and Albert Einstein both bear testimony to that. Both dropped out of school early, yet both became very successful. Someone with a positive attitude sees a silver lining to every cloud, but losers only see the cloud. Attitude is closely linked to what you focus on, or what some call "perspective." You can look for the good or you can look for the bad, but either way you will find what you are looking for. The Bible says, "He who seeks, finds." (Matthew 7:8) I once heard a saying that was used by the American Construction Battalion during World War II which I thought epitomised a positive mental attitude. During the war, especially during the island hopping campaign in the Pacific, the Americans captured island after island, which were heavily defended by the Japanese. The objective was to push the Japanese back to their homeland. Casualties were heavy on both sides, as some of the ferocious battles lasted much longer than anticipated by the American high command. Once an island had been taken, and the island declared secure, the Americans would move on to their next objective. One of the purposes of the Construction Battalion was to repair airfields and construct barracks for the troops. The C.B. (nicknamed Seabees) were so efficient that in some cases, as was the case on Iwo Jima, they had the airfield functioning even before the island was taken. Often the construction workers would come under enemy fire from snipers, yet they persevered. Their slogan was, "We do the difficult immediately; the impossible takes a little longer." And when asked to perform a particular task, their response was usually summed up in two words: "Can do."

But having a positive mental attitude isn't just confined to the battlefield; it's also being able to look for the good in a situation when things go wrong in our daily lives. Napoleon Hill said, "Within every adversity, setback, or disappointment lies the seed of greater or equal benefit." But we have to look for it. Often we are too busy focusing on the calamity that we don't see the benefit. It's not that it's not there, but we're not going to see what we don't focus on. Obviously there are certain exceptions to this, such as the death of a loved one, but in the vast majority of cases we tend to focus only on the calamity without even thinking that there could be a silver lining to the cloud. And if we don't see it, we aren't going to take advantage of it. Very often a person's failure can be the beginning of something better. For example, when I was looking to buy another house a few years ago, a great offer came up; it was exactly what I was looking for and it was in a very sought-after area. The price was unusually low because it had been re-possessed and it was only just on the market. So I quickly put in an offer which my estate agent and I thought would certainly be accepted by the seller. As it turned out, someone else's offer was accepted instead. I couldn't believe it. I thought that after months of searching, things had finally gone my way. I was wrong and very disappointed. So I just had to get over it and keep going. I kept looking and putting in a few more offers, but I wasn't getting anywhere. Then another good deal came up, but I was outbid. That one wasn't to be either. I was beginning to wonder if I would ever get a house, but I kept looking anyway. Then I decided to go and view a house that had been on the market for some time but that I didn't have great expectations for, but I thought I should keep looking just for the sake of gaining experience. When I got there I couldn't believe it; I had no idea that it was as good as this. I didn't even realise that this was the housing development referred to in the advertisement. It was also a bargain price. So I quickly put in an offer and it was accepted. I was delighted, and also glad that my previous offers had been turned down, because if I had gotten one of the previous houses then I wouldn't have gotten this one. I had found "the greater or equal benefit" to my previous disappointments. Sometimes when I think back, I think of how fortunate I was that I didn't get one of those previous houses. One of them needed a lot of money spent on it (with money I didn't have), but the one I bought was in walk-in condition. I also realised that sometimes we get mad at God because we don't get what we think we want, but it can sometimes be because He has something better for us instead.

Another example is when someone gets made redundant. Being made redundant can seem like a calamity, but many people have used this as an opportunity to start something new, such as their own business. Many people say they wish they had done this years ago. Such a person has found "the seed of greater or equal benefit" to the apparent setback or disappointment. And as time goes by, they might even look upon the redundancy as a blessing in disguise. What do you focus on when adversity strikes? Is your attitude positive or negative? Sometimes you can't seem to find any good in the situation, but realise that it's strengthening you and building your character. Sometimes that alone can be the silver lining to the cloud. Other times it can be the lessons learned from the experience that provide a greater or equal benefit.

The other important thing to realise is that whether we respond positively or negatively, it's habit forming. If we respond positively once, then we make it easier for ourselves to respond positively again. Eventually, when we respond positively often enough, we don't even have to think about it, we just do it automatically because it has become a habit. Unfortunately, the same principle holds true for responding negatively, and it usually leads to a downward spiral of pessimism. So we need to consciously make an effort to respond positively, until it becomes part of our subconscious and part of our character. Our character then determines our destiny.

DON'T BE ATTACHED TO AN OUTCOME

As long as we allow our happiness to depend on other people's actions or circumstances beyond our control, we will not be truly happy, because our happiness will be conditional. We will be up and down like a yo-yo because certain events happened or a certain person did something, or they didn't do something they were supposed to. Some people are happy as long as a certain person behaves in a certain way, or as long as things go as planned, or as long as the weather is good, or as long as their football team wins. But if we allow circumstances to control our attitude, then we will feel like victims, tossed about here, there, and everywhere, by the circumstances of life, unless we choose to take control and realise that our attitude is a choice and so is happiness.

Of course, there will be things that happen that we don't like, but unless we take control, instead of letting things control us, we will feel powerless and helpless. Think of your attitude as being like a rock on the seafront. That rock withstands all the battering from the severe weather, year in and year out. But the rock doesn't change according to the battering it receives; neither does it run away. It stands firm, no matter what happens to it. So should we also strive to stand firm with our attitude. I know it is easier said than done, but we should at least be striving towards it. Then we will be happier!

for BELIEF

Belief is a very powerful force that has the power to work miracles in our lives. It doesn't matter if what we believe is true or false; if we believe it, then belief alone can create it. If you don't believe it, then it probably won't happen. It's as simple as that. But before we go any further, this is not some kind of magic; it is simply how our mind works. As Dr. Joseph Murphy explains in his book The Power of Your Subconscious Mind, our subconscious mind is like a magnet; it creates conditions, situations, and events according to belief. For example, an athlete who believes in his heart that he is going to win usually wins. Belief alone can cause them to win. If they believe they are going to lose, they will probably lose. It's not a case of "because we don't win that we don't believe," it's because we don't believe that we don't win. Belief must come first because belief is creative.

When something is sincerely believed, the subconscious aligns everything else with this belief in order to bring it about. The subconscious has powers that we consciously know nothing of. The subconscious doesn't care about facts; it responds and creates according to belief, even if the facts are contradictory to what we believe. For example, if you believe that people will be hostile towards you, they probably will be. Subconsciously you may act differently toward them, and this will create the actual circumstances to back up what you believe, whereas these same people might have been very friendly toward you if your beliefs had been different. Most people, through a lack of knowledge, think that the facts are more important, but what they fail to realise is that your subconscious mind can create "facts," even if it wasn't a fact to begin with.

Believing something causes you to have a certain state of mind, similar to faith. But you cannot fake belief, you cannot pretend to believe, because then you don't really believe in your heart and you won't see the results. Your subconscious knows deep down what you believe, and responds accordingly.

Belief also causes an emotional response in our bodies, depending on what is believed. But what is believed is not always the truth. For example, suppose you were walking along the road, and just as you passed the driveway to a house you noticed a big vicious-looking dog sitting in the garden. Suddenly it notices you and comes running and growling straight towards you. Quite understandably you experience fear and your heart is pounding. But suddenly it stops in its tracks, about six feet away from you. You realise that it is on a chain and cannot come any further. Phew! You breathe a sigh of relief and wipe the sweat from your brow. You're completely safe! Your heartbeat goes back to normal and you thank your lucky stars.

So why did you experience fear when all the time you were completely safe and the dog could do you no harm? That was a fact. The reason you experienced fear was because of what you believed. You believed in your heart that you were in extreme danger, and that was what your subconscious responded to, even although there was no truth in it.

Suppose, on another occasion, one of your friends was in the hospital with some kind of illness and suddenly you got a phone call during the night and the doctor said, "I'm sorry to inform you, but your friend's condition has deteriorated rapidly within the last few hours." Obviously this would cause you to be in a state of panic and alarm as a result of hearing this. But supposing a few hours later the doctor called back and said, "Mr.— I'm really sorry, but I've gotten you mixed up with someone else. Your friend is absolutely fine and has made an excellent recovery. I do apologise." How would you feel then? Obviously relieved and overjoyed! (Different emotions as a result of different beliefs.)

The facts hadn't changed, only your beliefs. You also realise that the emotions of panic and alarm that you experienced earlier were a subconscious response to a false belief. So, suppose that you believe negative things about yourself just now, such as "I'm going to fail," or "other people are superior," or "I could never do what he's doing," your subconscious would also respond to these beliefs and would help bring them about.

So why not start believing positive things about yourself, and tell yourself, "I'm going to succeed" and "I'm as good as anyone else." And if you tell yourself something often enough, eventually you will start to believe it. So, if you started telling yourself that you deserve success and that you were born to succeed, do you think that would change the results you got in your life? Of course it would. Remember, different beliefs create different results. Facts have nothing to do with it. The only time the facts have anything to do with it is when the facts are believed. For example, during a football match, the team who believes they are the better side and believes they are going to win probably will, whereas a team who believes they are inferior to the other side and that they have a slim chance of winning, will probably lose. Either way, belief creates results. What do you believe? Do you believe you are going to win? Do you believe you are worthy of success? If not, then you need to change your beliefs. Don't make the mistake of trying to change the results while holding onto negative beliefs. The beliefs must change first, not the other way about.

I am reminded of the true story of a man who qualified

to go on a cruise. He was a sales person, and the organisation had laid on a special promotion as a reward for making the most presentations in a certain period of time. Everyone in the organisation was entitled to go in for it, but only a few would qualify, as there was only a limited number of spaces.

Many people tried to qualify, but many people also failed to meet the requirements. The people who did qualify were later asked to come up on stage and be recognised for their achievements. And I'll never forget what this one guy said. He said, "I'm very grateful to be going on this cruise, but as soon as it was announced, I just knew that I'd get there. I didn't know how, but I just knew deep down that I'd get there." And I thought to myself, "That's awesome! How could someone be as confident as that?" I mean, here we are (or should I say, here I am), struggling to try and qualify, and I didn't think I had a hope in hell of going on that cruise (although it would be nice if it happened), and that guy had the confidence to believe that he would go. How could he be that confident? Where did he get it from?

Well, as time went by, I began to realise that the reason he went on the cruise was because he believed he would. And the reason I didn't go was because I believed I would fail. He believed he would succeed, and did. I believed I would fail, and did. Different beliefs, different results. In both cases, our subconscious responded to our beliefs.

So, by now you might be thinking, "That's all very well, but suppose I want to believe but cant. What do I do then?" Well, what I would recommend is to change what goes into your mind. You cannot consciously change a belief, because beliefs are held at a subconscious level. But by reading regularly from a positive thinking book, it will start to change what's in your subconscious. It will change you from the inside out, and will gradually start to get rid of old negative beliefs and replace them with positive beliefs.

Another form of belief is having faith. Faith is belief. Faith is believing when there is little or no evidence to back up what you believe. For example, when I was writing my first book, I had to believe in what I was doing. I had to believe that my book would get published and that all my efforts weren't going to be in vain. In spite of the odds being stacked against me and receiving some discouraging comments, I had to believe that I would succeed, and I had to mentally "flush" discouraging remarks. Some people would say, "You're putting a lot of work into something that might not even come to anything," or "You might not even get published at all," which was true. Both comments were valid and true, but they were negative. Remember, your subconscious doesn't care about facts; it responds to belief. So I had to mentally hold firm to my belief, and I had to align my actions with my belief (which was to write the book).

The power of faith (and belief) is also clearly demonstrated in the Bible. Jesus said, "Because you have so little faith. I tell you the truth, if you have faith as small as a mustard seed, you can say to this mountain, 'Move from here to there' and it will move. Nothing will be impossible for you." (Matthew 17:20-21).

When the apostle Peter got out of the boat and walked on the water, he was able to do so because of his faith and belief in Christ. But as soon as he started to doubt, he started to sink. The Bible says, "But when he saw the wind he was afraid, and beginning to sink, cried out, 'Lord, save me!' Immediately Jesus reached out his hand and caught him. 'You of little faith,' he said, 'why did you doubt?'" (Matthew 14:30-31).

Notice how there was a direct relation between what Peter was able to do (walk on water) and his level of belief. As soon as his belief changed, so did the results.

Belief can also mean the difference between being healed and not being healed. This is further demonstrated in the book of Luke when Jesus said, "Don't be afraid; just believe, and she will be healed." (Luke 8:50) If you don't believe that something is possible, you mentally close off all possibilities for making it happen. Your subconscious then cannot work in your favour because your subconscious responds to your level of belief. Remember that your subconscious, which responds to belief, is the builder of your body, and is responsible for healing you.

Belief affects us in more ways than you might think. The clothes you wear have an effect on yourself image and how you feel about yourself. What you believe about the clothes you wear will affect how you feel about yourself. For example, if you believed that only professional people wore suits, every time you put on a suit you would feel professional. Your subconscious would respond to your level of belief about the clothes, and you would act accordingly. If you have a tattoo, whatever you believe about the tattoo will be operating at a subconscious level, and you will act accordingly. I once heard a chaplain speak about his visit to a prison where he was speaking to some of the inmates. He noticed that one of the prisoners had a tattoo that said, "Born to Lose."

He wasn't surprised that he had ended up in prison, because the tattoo had become a self-fulfilling prophecy. When you write something down, you write on the mind. This is then looked upon as a goal for the subconscious, and it acts accordingly. Remember, the subconscious takes everything literally and does not take a joke.

for CHANGE

Change is something that affects all of us whether we like it or not. We may be resistant to change and try to fight it, or we may welcome it, but we can't stop it. Everything is changing all the time. The only constant is change itself. The twentieth century saw more changes than all the previous centuries combined. 1903 saw the advent of flight when the Wright Brothers first took to the air. Then, just sixty-six years later, man landed on the moon.

When World War II broke out in 1939, bi-planes were still in active service. By the time the war had ended just six years later, the jet engine had been invented and jet fighters had seen combat. Today we also benefit from the use of mobile phones and computers. No longer do you have to have to find a payphone in the street; you simply go into your pocket and pull out your mobile phone, wherever you are.

The internet is another major development, which at the beginning of the twentieth century would have been un-thinkable. Today people can buy things online and have them delivered to their door, saving them valuable time. We can also communicate electronically with people in other countries through the use of E mail and text messaging. Gone are the days when we used to rely on carrier pigeons.

But this doesn't mean that all change has been positive.

For example, the decline in moral standards, such as an increase in violence and pornography on TV, is a negative aspect of change.

We cannot stop this either, but we can control whether we watch TV or not. But in respect to positive change, such as changes in fashion and technology, we either accept change or fall behind. The people who get ahead are the ones who take advantage of positive change and adapt to it. For example, if one supermarket decides to introduce home shopping, free of charge, the other supermarkets really have to do the same or else they're going to get left behind. But there is also another aspect to change, and that is the ability to change ourselves.

This doesn't mean that there is anything wrong with us, but none of us are anywhere near, or will ever come close to, reaching our full potential. We all have plenty of room for improvement. People who reject this or think that they don't need to change because they know all they need to know are the people who usually never rise above mediocrity. On the other hand, people who succeed are willing to admit their faults and their shortcomings and are therefore open-minded to learning and becoming better. In other words, they are teachable. Actually, the ability to change should be viewed as a gift, not as a burden, because if we were unable to change, we would be limited in what we could achieve, and we would be stuck where we are. It would also mean that people with inferiority complexes could never develop self confidence, and people with a negative attitude could never become positive thinkers. But fortunately this is not the case, because by changing what goes into our minds and changing what we tell ourselves, we can change our self image. The mind will accept whatever we put into it. This alone is good news. We can, to a certain degree, choose the type of person we want to become. If we are introverted, we can become more extroverted. If we lack confidence, we can become confident. God did not create some people to be greater or more confident than others. He did not say to himself, "Now this person will be super confident, well liked and admired, and this other person will be lacking confidence and not so popular."No, not at all. While it is true that some people may feel like a failure or a nobody, there is actually no truth in it. Why?

Because of the ability to change. If a person feels like a failure or a nobody, they need to realise that they were not born that way and they do not need to stay that way. The playing field is level for all of us when we are born. Self confidence is something which is either gained or lost as we go through life.

The self confident person has developed self confidence because they have chosen to respond positively to situations and events, and it is a choice, whereas a person with an inferiority complex has usually responded negatively to situations and events. In both cases, there has been a progressive increase or decrease in self confidence as a result. But fortunately God has provided us with the ability to change if we are willing to put the effort in. I have seen so many examples now of people who changed their self image by changing what went into their minds that it leaves no doubt in my mind that everybody has the potential to be great. And I mean absolutely everybody.

Take the example of the shy and introverted person who viewed themselves as a failure. If they were able to overcome their shyness and become self confident, then obviously they had believed a lie about themselves in the first place. But because of the ability to change, they were able to prove their original beliefs false, and realise the "truth" about themselves.

Maxwell Maltz, author of Psycho Cybernetics, refers to this as "self realisation," meaning that when a person changes his or her self image (or beliefs), they haven't suddenly developed some magical qualities that weren't there before, because these qualities have been there all the time. The difference is that they now believe it. In other words, they believe now what they didn't believe before.

When it comes to change, there are basically two groups of people. There are people who moan and complain about their situation but don't want to do anything about it, and there are people who are hungry for change because they are so dissatisfied with their lives that they're just looking for an opportunity to get ahead. The first group we can do nothing for. We can't help people who don't want to help themselves. But the second group we can help, because of their willingness to change. Like it or not, success involves change. It involves not only changing what we do, but also changing ourselves. It involves changing our beliefs, our habits, and what goes into our minds. We need to change how we think.

To attempt to succeed without being willing to change is to set yourself up for failure. There is no such thing as something for nothing. No pain, no gain. But change can also mean changing strategies or the way we do things. We always need to keep an open mind and realise that there can sometimes be a better way of doing things. This could be changing the way we provide a service or market a product. It could be changing the way we answer the telephone or the way we approach prospective buyers. It could be anything. But what we want to avoid is mentally getting into a rut, where we become close-minded to change. This doesn't mean that we should automatically accept every new idea that comes along, either, but it does mean that we should check it out and realise that there could be a better way.

You've probably heard people say things such as, "But that's the way we've always done it." This is mediocre thinking at its best. Such a person has usually conditioned themselves to stay average by slamming the door shut on any opportunities for advancement and limiting themselves in the process. It's similar to the experiment with the fleas in a jar. What happens is fleas are put into a jar and the lid is put on it (with air holes in the lid). The fleas, by nature, could normally jump much higher than the jar, but because the lid is on, that's as high as they can jump. So for twenty one days, the fleas are kept like this. Jumping up and down, but only as high as the lid permits. Then suddenly the lid is taken off and the fleas are now free to jump as high as they want. But do the fleas now jump much higher because the lid is off? No, they don't; they actually jump the exact same height as when the lid was on, because that's how they've been conditioned. Even although there's nothing stopping them and they have the ability to go as high as they want, they don't do it because that's as high as they believe they can go.

Unfortunately, the same thing has happened to many of us in our lives. We may not be stuck in a jar with a lid, but we have a "psychological lid" as a result of negative conditioning, and we allow negative beliefs to limit us. I often wonder how many opportunities are missed because of our conditioning. We will probably never know, but what we can do is change our conditioning by changing what goes into our minds. If our minds are "conditioned," they can also be re-conditioned.

I am also reminded of the story of the caterpillars that were used in a similar experiment. What happened was several caterpillars were put on a table and arranged so that they formed a circle. They were put nose to tail, all the way around so that they were almost touching each other, and they were left. This left a space in the middle of the circle where there was some food for the caterpillars. If the caterpillars wanted the food, which was very close to them, all they had to do was to break the formation and go into the middle and eat it. But that's not what happened. What did happen was that each one continued to follow the other and none of them broke out of the circle. As a result, they all died of starvation because none of them had the creativity to break out of their routine and get the food.

Yes, there was plenty of food there for them, and it was easily within their grasp, but they let their conditioning become their downfall. I often wonder how many people have let their conditioning become their downfall. Remember, the words we speak, whether positive or negative play a huge part in our conditioning, but we can change our conditioning any time we want. (I will cover this in more detail later in the book.) Why choose negative conditioning when you can just as easily choose positive conditioning? Some people might say, "But that's just the way I am" or "I can't help the way I am," but by speaking those very words they are actually programming themselves to stay that way. Not only that, but it is also denying responsibility for our thoughts and actions. When you deny responsibility, then you never will change. Remember that when you deny responsibility, you give away your power to the situation. When you do that, you're enslaved by it and it controls you, thus you invite mediocrity and failure. Instead, why not change what you tell yourself and realise that you DO have the power to change! Break free from the self-imposed prison you have created for yourself! When you change what you tell yourself, you will begin to change your conditioning; when you change your conditioning, you will change your self image and your lifestyle!

for DREAM

Do you know what you want out of life? That's a thought provoking question, isn't it? Where are you headed? That's another thought provoking question. If someone was to wake you up in the middle of the night and say, "What do you want out of life," would you be able to tell them instantly, or would you need to think about it? The reason it is tough is because the vast majority of the population don't even think about it. Most people are so caught up in the stress of day-to-day living that they lose sight of what they really want out of life. Yes, they are busy, but instead of their work being the means to an end, it becomes an end in itself.

Now, if you love what you do, that's great, and there's nothing wrong with that, but if you don't like what you do, and you are doing it just for a pay cheque, then realise that this may just be a temporary vehicle to get you to your dreams. Many people fail to achieve greatly in life because they think too small. Instead of dreaming big, they reduce their dreams to the size of their income level. If they don't have the financial resources to achieve what they want just now, they say things like, "And where am I going to get the money to achieve that?" The problem is that their thinking is the wrong way around. They reduce their dreams to the size of their income level, instead of expanding their income to the size of their dreams. Only when they focus on expanding their income will they attract opportunities to bring it about; otherwise they'll limit themselves and close off any opportunities to increase their income. Imagine not having to worry about bills ever again and not having to make mortgage payments anymore because your house is paid for. Imagine being able to pay cash for a new car and to make your choice based on what you want rather than what you can afford. Imagine being financially secure for the rest of your life!

But having a dream doesn't have to be something material; you may want to raise money for a charitable cause. Have you ever seen heartbreaking pictures of people in third world countries who don't have enough food or medicine or clean water? Think about what you could do if your income was ten times what it is just now! Money simply gives us more choices. There's nothing worse than wanting to give but not being able to, or wanting to do something but your finances won't allow it. You may love to travel but can't get away as often as you would like, either because of a lack of finances, or being tied to a job. Maybe you love flying and would love to take flying lessons or even own your own aircraft. Maybe you would like to spend more time sun-bathing in a hot country. Perhaps you would like to own a holiday home in that country. It could be that you simply want to have more free time to spend with your loved ones, but you need to have more money in order to buy back your time. Imagine being able to choose what you do every day and choose your own schedule instead of being answerable to a boss. The possibilities are almost endless.

While there's nothing wrong with wealth or material possessions, there is something wrong when they become more important than our families, or people in general. There is something wrong when money becomes number one in our life, and takes the place of God. But that doesn't have to be the case, because it's a choice that we personally make and we alone are responsible for. Interestingly, the Bible does not condemn money itself; it only condemns the love of money, which is a form of idolatry. It says, "For the love of money is a root of all kinds of evil. Some people, eager for money, have wandered from the faith and pierced themselves with many griefs." (1 Tim 6:10).

Although God wants us to prosper, He is also warning us about loving money to the extent that we cast Him aside and make some foolish choices. Many people have tried in vain to get the life they want by trampling over other people, and they have failed. But God promises us that if we do things His way, we will prosper. "But seek first his Kingdom and his righteousness, and all these things will be given to you as well." (Matthew 6:33) So, what has all of this got to do with our dreams? Well, quite a lot actually, because if we don't get our foundations right from the start, then we are doomed to failure. We need to have our foundations strong by building our house on a rock, rather than on sand. American business guru Dexter Yager said that the higher you want to go, the stronger and deeper your foundations need to be, which is absolutely true. But getting back to the original questions, "Do you know what you want?" and "Where are you headed?" If what you want doesn't match up with where you're headed, then you need to change course, because if you keep doing what you're doing, then you're going to keep getting the same results. You can't expect the results to change if you're not willing to make some changes. It would be similar to a ship leaving England for New York, and at the beginning of the voyage the captain realises he's a few degrees off course and he thinks to himself, "A few degrees isn't much; everything looks alright just now," and still expects to get to his destination. He may want to get to New York, but he may be headed for Mexico. Therefore, if he wants to get New York, he won't get there unless he changes course. Only then will what he wants match up with where he's headed. So where are you headed? What do you want? Do they match up? Are your dreams and goals written down? Do you have pictures of your dreams hanging up where you can see them every day? Do you have a plan to achieve them? Are you working on that plan right now? Realise that when you have something written down or have pictures of it where you see it every day, all this is being absorbed by your mighty subconscious, which is your goal-seeking mechanism, and it will start to take you in that direction. But you must be able to see it, because out of sight means out of mind.

You will also activate the law of attraction, which means that your most dominant thoughts will eventually become your reality. This is very often what happens in a person's life, whether they succeed or fail. The successful person uses this law to their advantage by writing down what they want, saturating their mind with thoughts of success, developing a plan of action, and taking action. They also use positive affirmations to help speak it into existence. But the person who fails is usually ignorant of the law of attraction and doesn't realise that this same law applies to them. Therefore, they never usually think about dreams or goals, because they are too focused and too caught up in the trivia of daily living. Because they focus on trivia, they get more trivia in their life. Your mind works a bit like a camera; a camera can't be focusing on something far away and something up close at the same time. One will always be at the expense of the other. In a similar way, when you focus on daily trivia, the latest gossip, and what's happening in the news, you won't be focusing on your dreams. And a person who focuses on their dreams and is actively involved in a worthwhile project will have no time to focus on daily trivia, the latest gossip, or what's happening in the news. One or the other will dominate.

The person who fails is normally in the habit of using negative words such as, "I'll never be rich," or "It's alright for them, they were lucky," and they program themselves for failure. The law of attraction is neutral and can cause you to succeed or fail depending on how you program your mind. Speak only words of success. Never let words of doubt or failure be heard on your lips, as you will attract what you continually talk about. You may need to change some of your habits, because it's our habits that have got us to where we are today. Some people have all the trappings of success and look good on the outside but are hurting on the inside. They may be very good at what they do and have everything they want financially, but they are so busy working that they don't have a life. What good is it to have money if you hardly ever see your husband or wife? What good is money if you hardly ever see your kids? Of course, if you were to ask people what was more important to them, they would reply that it was their families (or hopefully they would). Yet if you would look at what percentage of the day they spend making money and what percentage they spend with their families, this very often paints a very different picture. Of course we all need to make money, but if things get too unbalanced, other areas of our lives will start to suffer.

Time and money are very closely related. Whatever our dreams are usually requires more time or money (or both) to achieve them. But here's the catch: we first have to give up whatever it is that we want. If we want more money, we need to invest more money. We may have to pay for seminars, books, and motivational materials and the like. If we want more time, we need to give up some of our time just now so that we can enjoy more time later on. This usually involves sacrifice and discipline. You may have to cut down slightly on the social life just now so that you can enjoy time and money freedom later on. Remember, no pain, no gain. I say cut down slightly, not completely, because we always need to keep a sensible balance between work and play. You may need to give up a couple of evenings a week. But we still need to be crystal clear about what we want, otherwise how will we know when we've achieved it? It reminds me of the story of the guy going to purchase a train ticket. He walks up to the desk at the station and says, "Could I have a first class ticket?" The person behind the desk says, "Of course, where are you going?" And he says, "Well, I don't know, I haven't really thought about it yet," and the person behind the desk says, "Well, in that case, it doesn't really matter which train you take." Now, we may laugh at the stupidity of that, but many of our lives are like that. Many of us don't know where we are going and have never really thought about it, but we're still hoping to be successful. Only when we know where we are going and what we want will we have a chance of getting there. We need to have a clearly defined dream and a plan to achieve it. This also gives our subconscious mind something definite to work on. The more specific the instructions to our subconscious mind, the better, and the more chance of making it a reality. You could liken it to the guy going to purchase the train ticket; he now knows where he's going, so there's a lot better chance he's going to get there.

You might have a goal to own rental property, but rather than just say, "I want to own rental property," it would be better to be more specific. For example, you might say, "I want to own six rental properties by a certain date." Also, you need to write things down, such as what size of properties? How many bedrooms? In which town or country would you like to own them? How many square feet? Do you have pictures of them? Will you own them outright? Why not get a picture of them and write these things next to it and put it somewhere you will see it every day? You might even want to write down the amount of rent you expect to receive from each one. You might also want to write "debt free" next to them as well. But that's just an example, and it's completely up to you which goals you set.

Some people might say, isn't that a bit materialistic? Well, remember that God created the material world, but it's what we do with what we've got that matters. It's what we do with what we've got that God will judge us on. The Bible tells us, "From everyone who has been given much, much will be demanded; and from the one who has been entrusted with much, much more will be asked." (Luke 12:48) This doesn't mean that there's anything wrong with ambition; the

Bible only condemns selfish ambition (see Phil 2:3-4). There's a big difference between ambition for own selfish desires and ambition which will benefit mankind. If there was no ambition then nothing would have been invented, man would never have stepped on the moon, and we would still be living in caves. Of course we need ambition! It's ambition that inspired great inventors such as Edison and great pioneers such as the Wright brothers. It's ambition that has caused technological breakthroughs and great engineering feats. Ambition knows no limits! You are only limited by your imagination.

It's a well known success principle that when you help enough other people get what they want, what you want comes automatically. You may or may not have heard of Joel Osteen, Pastor of Lakewood Church in Houston, Texas. He frequently speaks on the God channel and inspires millions of people around the world. To me, he epitomises success, because not only has he greatly achieved in terms of his own personal achievements, but he also has a strong desire to help other people. That's what true success is all about— helping other people. Contrary to what some Christians believe, we do not glorify God by living in poverty or mediocrity. We were created to excel, while helping other people to excel. If we don't excel, then how can we help other people excel? We can't.

There's nothing wrong with having a lot of money, fancy cars, nice big houses, or whatever, as long as we realise that these things are not an end in themselves, but simply by-products of success. Neither should we place our trust in wealth or material objects. The Bible says, "He who trusts in his riches will fall, but the righteous will thrive like a green leaf." (Prov 11:28) Therefore, we need to place our trust in God at all times and stay obedient to Him; then our wealth and material possessions will fall into their proper perspective. The more we achieve, the more we should be doing to help others. The irony is that the more we help others, the more we will achieve! So dream big and keep your dream in front of you!

for EMOTIONAL CONTROL

If we want to become successful, we need to learn to control our emotions and not let them control us. We need to know the difference between positive and negative emotions and learn to practice and embrace positive emotions and avoid the negative. This is probably one of the hardest things we will ever do, because trying to stay positive when things are going against us is not easy. For example, every one of us has at some point experienced one or more of the following: fear, anger, greed, lust, jealousy, worry, self pity or even hatred.

Obviously there are many more, but these are just some examples of negative and destructive emotions that can cause us to fail if we let them control us. But just because you experience a negative emotion doesn't necessarily mean it's controlling you; it depends on how you respond to it. For example, you might experience fear, but instead of running from it, you do the opposite and face your fear. In that case, although you still experienced fear, you controlled it by acting in spite of it; whereas if you had avoided your fear, it would have controlled you. Therefore, your response will either be based on fear or courage, and your world will either expand or get smaller as a result. If you face your fears, your world expands, but if you avoid what you fear, your world gets smaller and you limit yourself.

People respond differently to different emotions, and it's a choice that we must personally make. For example, two different people may experience the exact same emotion, but one responds negatively and the other positively. For example, suppose two different people experience "disappointment" during a business venture. One person gives up and quits (letting disappointment control them), and the other one perseveres in spite of it. Their situation and circumstances could be exactly the same, but because of a different response, their outcome will be different. These two different responses might not seem very significant at the time, but long term it can mean the difference between success and failure, happiness and unhappiness, a good self image and a poor self image.

One person was controlled by disappointment but the other one controlled the disappointment. Someone might experience disappointment in a relationship and say, "That's it! I'm finished with relationships!" and turn down all future invitations to go out with someone else. Such a person, although they may be hurt, also deprive themselves of positive and happy experiences in the future because they let their past control their future. This may even lead to other negative emotions such as cynicism or self pity. Whereas someone who responds positively to the disappointment, although they may still need time to get over it, realises they cannot judge their future by their past, and that life must go on. Therefore they are still open to going out with other people in the future.

How we respond to negative emotions is also habit forming. A person who quits when faced with disappointment will probably quit other things in the future when the going gets tough again. This holds true whether it's in business, sports, a fitness club, or whatever, but someone who responds positively has also formed the habit of responding positively and has created an upward spiral of courage and self confidence. Because they responded positively once, they find it easier to respond positively again. They know that the best response to disappointment is persistence.

Fear is probably one of the biggest barriers to success that there is. For example, there is fear of getting out of our comfort zones and doing something new, fear of the unknown, fear of failure, fear of what other people might think, fear of having to face our fears, fear of being classed as different, and fear of other people, just to name a few. There is only one antidote to fear, and that is to take action. Taking action, although it is not always easy, will solve all of the above. Then you will be controlling fear, and it will lose its grip on you. But let's not forget the positive emotions, such as courage and faith. Faith is the opposite of fear. You cannot have both at the same time, because one cancels the other one out. Positive and negative emotions cannot exist simultaneously. Just as we want to avoid letting negative emotions control us, we also want to put into practice and base our actions on positive emotions. The ideal situation is for us to base all of our actions on positive emotions and never on the negative. Emotions such as love, faith, desire, romance, hope, and enthusiasm are some of many of the powerful positive emotions. It might be a good idea to start asking yourself what emotion is behind each action you take or each decision you make. Our emotions are constantly driving our behaviour, even if we are not aware of it. Positive emotions lead to happiness and prosperity, but negative emotions lead to unhappiness and poverty.

But getting back to the emotion of fear, we can either face our fear with courage and faith that God is going to help us, or we can let fear control us and paralyse us. If we choose to respond with courage, then our self confidence grows, our fear diminishes, and a whole new world of opportunities opens up to us. But if we give in to it, then we become a slave to our fear, we lose self confidence, and we limit ourselves in terms of what we can achieve. Two different choices, and two extremely different results. I have written in more detail about emotions in my first book, "You are the problem, You are the solution" I also recommend reading Napoleon Hill's bestselling book, Think and Grow Rich, which explains in detail about the subconscious mind and the emotions.

But remember, there is nothing wrong with experiencing fear; it's our response to fear that matters. In many cases it is very normal and natural to experience fear. Fear is our internal warning system to let us know that we're in danger. Without this warning system we could and probably would come to far more harm than we do. For example, if we woke up in the middle of the night and our house was on fire, the fear of being trapped inside a burning house could cause us to get out and save our life. Or if we were walking on the very top of a skyscraper on a windy day, fear of falling off might cause us to keep away from the edge. In both of these cases fear is healthy and could be classed as "normal fear." But there is also another type of fear which is counter-productive and is known as "abnormal fear." This type of fear does not help us, but hinders us and prevents us from getting what we want, unless we choose to face it and overcome it. For example, you might be a sales person and have a list of people you're afraid to call because of fear of rejection or ridicule. This type of fear will stand between you and your dreams if you allow it to control you, whereas you could respond positively to the fear by taking action and phoning the people you're afraid to phone. Not only would this open the door to you becoming successful, but the fear itself would start to disappear.

The Bible also tells us, "There is no fear in love. But perfect love drives out fear." (1 John 4:18) Therefore, if you are practicing the emotion of love, it is impossible to be afraid at the same time. Maybe that's one of the reasons Jesus told us to love our enemies? Not only is it the right thing to do, but we ourselves will benefit. It's impossible to experience any kind of negative emotions while you're operating in the mindset of love. Love can, and will, only do good. It actually benefits the giver more than the recipient.

Some people hate their enemies, but not only is this wrong, it is also pointless, because hatred affects us a lot more than the other person. It is impossible to hate and be happy at the same time, yet if we hate our enemies we will still be susceptible to the emotion of fear, because both emotions are negative. You often find that one negative emotion is quickly followed by other negative emotions. This might sound strange, but behind hostility is fear. Fear is usually just beneath the surface of hatred, because subconsciously we are expecting hatred in return.

The Bible also tells us, "If anyone says 'I love God' yet hates his brother, he is a liar. For anyone who does not love his brother, whom he has seen, cannot love God, whom he has not seen." (1 John 4:20) You will find that the Bible gives instruction on practically every single emotion you can think of (positive and negative). The benefits of the positive and the consequences of the negative. If we follow the wisdom given to us, this will go a long way toward us becoming successful and will help us to control our emotions instead of letting them control us.

Another emotion that can stand in our way is frustration. Frustration, although negative, is a very normal emotion to experience, and is not always our fault. Many people experience frustration when everything seems to be going against them, or things don't go the way they hoped they would. The danger is that frustration can lead to anger or even self-pity and can end up causing people to quit. We may get involved in a business venture or some kind of project and experience frustration along the way. Disappointment usually precedes frustration. Someone we thought we could depend on lets us down. A contract we thought we were getting goes to someone else. Or just when success looked like it was within our grasp, everything goes wrong. Or we may be putting massive effort into something and making virtually no progress, at least not just now. All of these things can cause frustration. But once again, the answer to frustration lies in our own response and our own mental attitude. Do we let it control us or do we control it? The best response I know of can be summed up in one word: persistence.

Eventually persistence coupled with faith wears down all obstacles. But unfortunately not everyone persists and not everyone has faith. Some people have doubt instead of faith, and they quit. Some people respond to frustration with anger, and they quit. But each person will make their own choice and each person will determine their own destiny.

It's important to note here that the people who choose to persist (and succeed) also experience the same amount of frustration as anyone else. They may even experience anger too, but the big difference is in how they respond to these emotions. The positive response to frustration we have just covered, but in the case of anger, the positive response is not to let it out negatively (for example, cursing or complaining), but to use this energy in a positive way. For example, you may decide to do twice as much work as you did before, and adopt the "I'll show them!" mentality.

This extra release of energy will help to get rid of some of your anger, and you will also know that it's being directed toward a positive end, which will make you feel better.

Another thing that can cause us problems emotionally is when our conscious and subconscious minds are in conflict with each other. To understand that, we need to realise that the two different parts to the same mind perform different tasks. For example, when we decide to do or not to do something, that is conscious thinking. But our beliefs and emotions are subconscious and are far more powerful than our conscious minds. That's why we can't consciously get rid of fear, we need to take action. That's also why, if we feel guilt, no amount of conscious thinking will get rid of it.

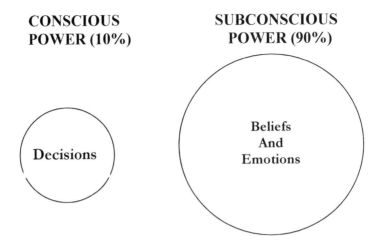

CONSCIOUS POWER (10%)

SUBCONSCIOUS POWER (90%)

Decisions

Beliefs And Emotions

Therefore, if we are in the habit of doing something which we believe isn't quite right, but we decide to keep on doing it anyway, we will have negative emotions as a result of that behaviour and we will run into problems. This could be a habit or behaviour which is unethical or immoral, but if we want to be happy and successful, then there has to be harmony between what we decide to do (conscious thinking) and what we believe is right (subconscious thinking). Our subconscious creates emotions according to what we truly believe in our heart. For example, if we believe a certain action is wrong and we do it, we will experience guilt, unhappiness, and a deterioration of our self image. But if we believe a certain action is right and we do it, we will experience very positive emotions such as courage, happiness, and a good self image. Only when we do what we believe in our heart is right will our emotions be positive. And only then will we be happy and successful. The problem usually lies in our own stubbornness, thinking that we know better, but we can't beat the mighty subconscious.

YOU CANNOT CONSCIOUSLY OVERRIDE EMOTIONS

Let me just explain what I mean by that. For example, a

person decides to start stealing. They were taught at a very young age that it is wrong to steal. Although they're an adult now, their inner belief is that it's wrong to steal, so if they like it or not, they'll suffer from guilt. What they tell themselves (consciously) makes no difference to their emotions and won't stop the guilt. They may try to ignore the guilt (which is impossible) or they may try to justify their stealing, but all of this conscious thinking makes no difference. The subconscious creates emotions according to what it believes (believing stealing is wrong) and therefore responds with corresponding emotions, such as guilt. Your subconscious will always respond to belief— end of story. That's why, if a person practices sexually immoral behaviour, they are not happy, because deep down they know it's wrong. If they like it or not, they will suffer from guilt and lust— making happiness impossible.

Therefore, if we want to be happy and successful, we must start listening to the quiet inner voice of our subconscious and be willing to submit to what we believe is right, rather than to fight against it. Only then will there be complete harmony in our minds, and only then will we be truly happy and successful.

for FORGIVENESS

To forgive is not always easy to do, but forgiveness actually benefits the giver much more than the recipient, because when you forgive someone you receive peace of mind, and you are the one who is liberated from the negative emotion of non-forgiveness (or hatred), not them.

Many people have fallen into the trap of thinking that when they forgive someone, they have done them a big favour, but in reality they have done themselves a bigger favour than anyone else. We must always remember that "unforgiveness" is a negative emotion which is extremely destructive to us. Not only does it destroy our peace of mind and our happiness, but there is growing evidence that negative emotions in general, long held and deep rooted, can destroy our physical bodies too. The Bible also bears testimony to this. For example, we are told, "A heart at peace gives life to the body, but envy rots the bones." (Proverbs 14:30). So if envy rots the bones, there's a high chance that other negative emotions, such as unforgiveness, won't do our bodies much good either. But if we really think about it, what actually is unforgiveness? Unforgiveness really is a form of hatred. To hold a grudge is to hate; to forgive is to love (or at least to show love). Forgiveness is actually love in action. I believe the old saying is true: "A grudge is always heavier for the person who holds it."

Some people allow one negative action by another person to cause them to resent or hate that person for the rest of their lives. Even if that person (the wrongdoer) has changed their ways, some people just simply won't forgive. And when that happens, we ourselves become wrong. The Bible says, "If your brother sins, rebuke him, and if he repents, forgive him. If he sins against you seven times in a day and seven times comes back to you and says, 'I repent,' forgive him." (Luke 17:3-4) Although this is easier said than done, God knows what's best for us and is well aware of the liberating power of forgiveness. Apart from anything else, it's also the right thing to do. How can we hope to be forgiven if we ourselves don't forgive? But since forgiveness is so closely related to love, we might do well to see what the Bible says about love: "Love is patient, love is kind. It does not envy, it does not boast, it is not proud. It is not rude, it is not self seeking, it is not easily angered, it keeps no record of wrongs." (1 Cor 13:4-5) Notice how it says, "It keeps no record of wrongs." I'm sure, if we're honest, this is something that we all struggle with at times. Some people keep a mental "scorecard" on other people to the point that they become judgmental and sometimes hypocritical.

No matter how much the "wrongdoer" has changed their ways, they still refuse to see them in a new light because they're blinded by the "scorecard" they're keeping on them. Obviously this leads to a situation where the unforgiver becomes the wrongdoer for not forgiving. They forget that they themselves do wrong, hoping for forgiveness, so what right do they have for keeping a "scorecard" on other people?

True forgiveness is when someone has wronged you and you act towards them as though it had never happened. You don't allow their "wrongs" to become a barrier between you and them. It takes a big person to do this, but it also takes a small person to hold a grudge. This is a choice that we all must make, because in life, conflicts are inevitable, but it's how we deal with them that determines if we are happy or not. Un-forgiveness and happiness cannot co-exist. Therefore, from that point of view alone, it makes sense to forgive.

But another aspect of forgiveness is the forgiveness we seek from others, when we ourselves are the wrongdoers. This is something that we have no control over, because we cannot control the thoughts or actions of other people. Some people forgive and some don't, and we simply have to accept that. We can do our part and apologise, but at the end of the day, whether they forgive us or not is their choice and their decision. This doesn't mean that God's laws about forgiveness don't apply to them; of course they do, but unfortunately some people have no regard for God's laws and, as a result, won't benefit from the liberating power of forgiveness. But if we ourselves are hoping to be forgiven by others for the wrong we have done, then we need to be in the habit of forgiving other people, because we reap what we sow (see Galatians 6:7). We cannot plant an apple tree and expect to reap oranges. If we plant an apple tree, then apples are exactly what we will get. Therefore, if we want to reap forgiveness, then we must first sow forgiveness. The Bible says, "Forgive and you will be forgiven." (Luke 6:37)

This law applies to anything, not just forgiveness. If we sow love, we will reap love. If we sow good will, we will reap good will. If we sow wickedness, we will reap wickedness. Some people go around sowing bitterness, hatred, and resentment and wonder why they're not reaping better results.

But there is also another type of forgiveness which is far more important than being forgiven by other people, and that is God's forgiveness. God's superiority in love, wisdom, and understanding becomes even more apparent when it comes to forgiveness. Society may not forgive, but God always does. There is nothing God won't forgive if we repent and ask for His forgiveness.

"Blessed are they whose transgressions are forgiven, whose sins are covered.
Blessed is the man whose sin the Lord will never
count against him."
(Romans 4:7-8)

If we have truly repented and changed our ways, God
won't even bring it up! Isn't that good news? I know it was
good news for me when I read it. So if you have done
something wrong, repented, asked God's forgiveness, and
people won't forgive you, don't worry about it. All that
matters is that God has forgiven you. I remember reading a
book about a person who was plagued with guilt over
something they'd done a long time ago, and even although
they had changed their ways and confessed their sins to God,
they kept beating themselves up about it. After reading
some of Scripture, it was almost as if God was saying to
them, "You keep bringing it up, but I don't." So we also
need to learn to forgive ourselves, otherwise we won't move
on.

I remember someone once saying, "But couldn't you
just live how you wanted and at the last minute, just before
you died, you could repent?" I also heard someone else
saying that they thought it didn't really matter about our
sins, or how we live our lives, because we will simply be
forgiven. Well, first of all, how do we know when our time is
up? We don't. Therefore we could come face to face with
God a lot sooner than we think. So, we need to repent before
it's too late. And secondly, God knows what's in our hearts
and minds. He knows our every thought and our true motives. "For the Lord searches every heart and understands
every motive behind the thoughts." (1 Chronicles 28:9) Not
only that, but if you're doing something which you believe
is wrong, you'll suffer from negative emotions and you
won't be happy. It's simply not worth it!

But I want to just leave you with one thought. I want
you to think about how great God's love and compassion is

for us. Let me just ask you a question: Is there anyone you would die for? The chances are, you would probably die for your husband or wife, your children, certain family members, or maybe your close friends. But what about someone you didn't really know? Would you die for them? What about someone who wasn't a very nice person, would you die for them? The Bible tells us, "Very rarely will anyone die for a righteous man, though for a good man someone might possibly dare to die. But God demonstrates his own love for us in this: While we were still sinners, Christ died for us." (Romans 5:7-8)

for GIVING

You will normally find that people who are truly happy and successful are people who are in the habit of giving. Success is always found in the giving, not in the taking. Some people think of success in terms of what they can get or what they've accumulated, but true success is measured by helping other people and by what we've contributed. Take, for example, someone who inherits a fortune but has a terrible attitude toward other people and doesn't know how to manage their money; would you class them as successful? Probably not. Or what about someone who looks good on the outside, has a nice big house in a good neighbourhood, with fancy cars, who possibly even has a title, but wasn't happy on the inside; would you call that success? Probably not. If you want to become successful, focus on helping other people, doing what's right, and improving yourself. Then everything else will fall into place.

So, how do we help other people, you might ask. We do it by giving of ourselves. We do it by helping them to achieve their dreams. We do it by giving our advice, our support, and our time. As long as we have achieved in that area ourselves, then we can help them to get there too. When we've helped enough other people achieve their goals, then we will automatically achieve ours. Network marketing is one such example of this. Unlike the corporate world where it's dog-eat-dog and people get ahead by trampling over people, this type of business is structured in such a way that the only way you can succeed is by helping other people to succeed first. If we don't help anyone, then we don't succeed; it's as simple as that. This makes it very unique. Sometimes you might find yourself in the position of giving people advice. Just for the sake of an example, let's imagine success being like a ladder. Imagine the ladder has ten rungs and the top rung is where your dreams are (rung ten). When you first started out, whether it was network marketing or any venture at all for that matter, you were at zero (not even on the ladder yet). But now you've been in the business for some time and gained some experience and you are currently on rung five. Well, that means you are qualified to help other people to get to rung five because you know exactly how to do it. It also means that your advice is going to be sound advice because you have the experience. You cannot yet advise people on how to get to rung six and above until you get there yourself. But as you climb further up the ladder and gain more experience, your knowledge and ability to give advice also increases. When you get to rung seven, you can now help other people get to rung seven, and so on. Someone once said that success is a bit like climbing a mountain; each time you go a bit higher, the view gets a bit better. The more people we help, the more successful we become.

Someone once gave a classic example of heaven and hell. In hell, they described a huge hall with a banquet in it. There was an extremely long table with lots of people seated on each side of it. On the table there was the most delicious food you could possibly think of. There was more food than anyone could eat. But ironically, the people sitting at the table were starving. The people there were in such pain, he had never seen such torment. He wondered, "How when there is such an abundance of food can these people be starving?" Then he noticed that the eating utensils were three feet long. Because they were so long, no one could manage to get the food into their mouths. Then he went to visit heaven. And to his utter amazement, he saw exactly the same kind of banquet, the same amount of food, the same amount of people, and the eating utensils were also three feet long. But the people there were very happy, they were all well fed, and he had never seen such happiness. And he asked one of them, "How do you manage to eat when those utensils are three feet long? And the man replied, "In hell, people try to feed themselves, but in heaven we reach over and feed each other."

Nature has an uncanny way of giving us back whatever we give out. Unfortunately, some people are in the habit of taking as much as possible and giving as little as possible, but this is a recipe for failure. "Give and it will be given to you." (Luke 6:38) Whatever you share multiplies, and whatever you withhold diminishes. If you want money, give money. If you want love, give love. If you want smiles, give smiles. If you don't believe me, just practice smiling at everyone when you're walking down the street. Okay, they may not all smile back, but remember you're sowing seeds, and what you reap doesn't always come from the same source. You may find that someone else smiles at you later on. Life is like looking into a mirror; what we give is what we get. If we take no interest in other people, avoid making eye contact, and don't make conversation, then that's exactly what we'll get in return. We are the ones who set the tone. By choosing the tone, we can literally determine what we will attract. You've probably heard the saying "To have a friend, you first must be a friend." We can't be waiting for other people to come to us first, because very rarely will it happen. A lot of other people are probably thinking the same thing and are waiting for us to come to them. So we must be first to give of ourselves, then people will respond accordingly.

Another important aspect of giving is what is often referred to as going the extra mile. This is when you give more than you are currently paid for. The extra mile will always pay dividends, long term. You will also stand out head and shoulders from the competition. Why? Because do you realise how rare quality service is today? You often hear people complaining about poor workmanship or people being unreliable.

Unfortunately, many people providing products and services are in the habit of giving just enough and no more, and taking as much as possible. So where does that leave you and I? Well, it provides us with a big opportunity to give people what they are looking for. Not only to give people what they are looking for, but to give them a little bit more than they expect. People who want to give as little as possible are very short-term thinkers, because as soon as you find out what their product or service is like, you're unlikely to go back. Not only that, but chances are that you'll probably tell other people. I remember a while back going to a takeaway shop that sold filled rolls. It didn't take me long to realise that there was a shop just a little bit further along the road that, for a few extra pence, gave you about double the helping that this shop was giving you. They also provided a friendlier service. Needless to say I immediately started going to the other shop. But the point is that I often wonder how many other people did the same thing. Probably quite a few. Word of mouth is very powerful and the word soon gets about. Do you really think that the amount of money that the first shop saved by giving you a small amount was worth what they lost in terms of customers who didn't go back? I don't think so. The problem was that they were too focused on one particular sale instead of the big picture. They might think they're saving money by giving you as little as possible initially, but what's going to happen after that? Will people be satisfied? Will they come back? What will they tell their friends? It's a sad fact that nine out of ten businesses fail in the first five years.

Whereas people who give you more than you expect, while it may cost them more money initially, know that this will be compensated for later on by increased sales and repeat business. They're also wise enough to know how powerful word of mouth is and they know that people don't mind paying if they're getting good value. In both situations people plant seeds. Some people plant money seeds while others plant poverty seeds. Eventually people will find out what our product or service is like, and the results will speak for themselves.

And last but probably the most important way of giving is giving back to God. This is what the Bible refers to as "Tithing," which means to give a tenth. Although we should be giving out of a sincere desire to help other people, God also promises us that the more we give, the more we get, and that giving is the key to abundance. Some people have fallen into the trap of thinking that the more they give, the less they will have for themselves. While this might seem logical, it's an illusion. Greed is one of the biggest causes of poverty that there is. If you don't believe me, just look at the state of countries where there is corruption and lawlessness.

But giving actually leads to prosperity (see Proverbs 11:25). This principle, like many others, requires faith. But remember, faith has no logic to it because faith is believing in the unseen. Faith is also believing when we don't understand. The problem is that most people operate out of logic instead of faith. If they can't see how it would be possible, they don't believe it. And as a result they keep themselves in a vicious cycle.

for HABITS

Habits are something that either make us or break us. We all have them, it's just a question of whether they're positive or negative— or, shall we say, constructive or destructive? Habits are what make the difference between success and failure. If you were to examine the life of a successful person and examine the life of an average person (I won't say failure, because I don't believe anybody is a failure), you would find that there was a vast difference in their habits. It has nothing to do with luck, as some might suggest, but it has everything to do with things like the words they speak, attitude, discipline, hard work, commitment, sacrifice, and a host of other things.

But first of all we need to ask ourselves what is the difference between a positive and negative habit? Well, for the most part, it's common sense. For example, we all know that smoking is bad for us, but not all habits are quite so obvious. Sometimes we have habits that we don't give as much thought to. Generally speaking, a positive habit is beneficial for all involved, causes positive emotions, and brings us closer to our goals. A negative habit is destructive, causes negative emotions, and takes us further away from our goals. Any habit that causes us to have negative emotions is a failure habit that needs to be broken. Our subconscious mind, which controls our emotions, is therefore an excellent guide in helping us to distinguish between a positive and negative habit. For example, if a habit was causing us to feel guilt, anger, or lust, then this is a failure habit which needs to be broken. But let's first of all look at habits which could be called "subtle habits."

Subtle because a lot of people don't give them much thought, because they seem trivial and unimportant. Therefore they might be fooled into thinking that they don't really matter and won't have much of an impact on their life. This is a big mistake, because one "little habit" may not seem like much, but one bad habit is enough to drag you down to failure. It doesn't matter if you're successful in every other area; one bad habit can sabotage your success. Therefore, lots of habits put together, over the long term, will make a massive difference in where you end up in life.

For example, consider the different "subtle habits" of person A and person B (below) and see who you think would be more successful in life:

PERSON A
- Disciplined
- Sets goals
- Controls what goes into his mind
- Reads positive thinking books
- Listens to motivational CDs
- Associates with positive, ambitious people who know where they're going in life
- Speaks positive words

PERSON B
- Undisciplined
- Has no goals
- Never even considers what goes into his mind
- Watches TV regularly and reads newspapers
- Associates with negative people who are going no-where fast
- Speaks negative words

These are just a few examples of probably many more subtle habits which can cause people to succeed or fail. Very often these habits can be the little difference that makes the big difference. But we also need to be aware of the more "obvious habits" if they're going to stand in the way of our success. For example, things such as drunkenness, drug abuse, sexual immorality, and pornography are all things that can and will cause us to fail. Such habits are illusions, and they trick us into failure because they promise one thing and deliver another. They might promise happiness, pleasure, or even escapism, but they actually enslave us and lure us into a false sense of happiness, causing failure and misery. Consequently, we lose sight of our dreams. Unfortunately, some people don't realise that what sometimes looks so good on the outside can actually be our downfall. Remember that trickery and deception are favourite instruments of the devil. "Your enemy the devil prowls around like a roaring lion looking for someone to devour." (1 Peter 5:8). The devil knows that you can't be successful or effective for God if you're enslaved by a destructive habit, therefore he'll go all out to make a destructive habit seem as inviting as possible in order to keep you locked into a vicious cycle.

But if we look at the habit of alcoholism, you may not be an alcoholic, but excessive drinking can still cause you to fail, even if you regard yourself as successful in other areas. Some people drink excessively to try and escape from reality or forget about their problems, but the problem with that is that their problems don't go away. In fact, things usually get worse when we try to run away from them. All we will have done is added another problem to our problems. And we will be less effective in dealing with our problems while under the influence of drugs or alcohol. The only way to deal with problems is to face them head on. But if you feel like your problems are too heavy a burden to bear on your own, why not seek help or advice from a support group or a qualified professional? Turning to drugs or alcohol, whether for pleasure or to escape problems, can and usually does lead to disastrous results, sometimes resulting in ruining our health, and even death. Don't get me wrong, I'm not saying that all alcohol is bad. There's nothing wrong with the occasional drink in moderation. The Bible doesn't condemn alcohol itself, but it condemns drunkenness. In other words, we need to be in control of alcohol, and not the other way around. God wants us to be in control of ourselves all the time and He wants to protect us from the dangers associated with alcohol abuse. I'm sure we can all remember times when we've said or done things we regret while under the influence of alcohol. Therefore, we need to make a choice between habits that will lead to success and habits which lead to failure. The Bible gives us clear warning about the kind of behavior that isn't acceptable to God. "The acts of the sinful nature are obvious: sexual immorality, impurity and debauchery; idolatry and witchcraft; hatred, discord, jealousy, fits of rage, selfish ambition, dissensions, factions and envy; drunkenness, orgies and the like. I warn you as I did before that those who live like this will not inherit the Kingdom of God." (Galatians 5:19-21).

Remember that God doesn't give you all these rules to punish you or make you unhappy. He does it because He loves you and wants to protect you. We think our road is the best road, but He has a far better road. A road which leads to happiness and success, but few people ever discover it. Sometimes this can be because of our own stubbornness and unwillingness to change; other times it can be because we lack the faith to believe what God is telling us. Sometimes we just simply don't believe that His way will be better. This is a grave mistake, and one I made myself before I became a Christian. Our biggest problem is our own thinking, when we think we know better. But our thinking can also be our biggest asset if we control what goes into our minds.

If you can just grasp hold of what I'm telling you, you'll save yourself years of pain and hardship. God cares about every single aspect of your life, including your finances, and

He wants to help you. And if anything is going to be detrimental to our success, He will warn us about it. For example, we are told, "drunkards and gluttons become poor." (Proverbs 23:21).

But drunkenness is only one of many "obvious" failure habits. Sexual immorality is also another major problem area which can cause us to fail. The emotion of sex is a very positive emotion, but it is sometimes confused with the negative emotion of lust. God wants us to enjoy sex, but only within the realms of marriage. We are all given free will; we can either choose God's way, which will lead us to getting the desires of our heart, or we can do things our own way and end up with a whole bunch of problems. Not only that, but if we do things our way, the negative emotion of lust will dominate our thinking, making true happiness and success impossible. Once again, this has everything to do with faith. Do you have faith that God's way will be better? Or do you doubt His promises, choose to stay in a rut, and maybe never discover what He has in store for you? Each choice leads to a different road, and each road leads to a different destination.

Other areas of sexual immorality include adultery, sexual unfaithfulness, and pornography. Such habits wreak havoc in a person's life, causing negative emotions such as guilt, fear, worry, anxiety, and depression, to name a few. All deadly emotions to our happiness and success. The Bible tells us, "Flee from sexual immorality. All other sins a man commits are outside his body, but he who sins sexually sins against his own body." (1 Cor 6:18) The Bible warns us that sexual sin is different from the rest, in that it will somehow have an adverse affect on our physical bodies. In other words, we can physically destroy ourselves through sexual sin.

Some habits are hard to break, to the point that they become addictions. When that happens, you become a slave to the habit and it becomes your master. It's master of your emotions, it's master of your time, it's master of your happiness, and in some cases, master of your money. The more we get, the more we want and the more we convince ourselves that we couldn't get by without them. But this is a lie; this is trickery and deception on a massive scale, because not only can we get by without them, it's the very key to happiness and success. The longer we've been addicted, the longer we'll have held the belief that we need it. But this is part of the problem; our belief system has been messed up and what we believe is false. Never forget that the devil is a liar and loves to deceive. The Bible says about the devil, "When he lies, he speaks his native language, for he is a liar and the father of lies. Yet because I tell the truth, you do not believe me! Can any of you prove me guilty of sin?" (John 8:44-45)

God speaks only the truth. So, who will you listen to? Who will you believe? Many times in the Bible Jesus starts with the words, "I tell you the truth." So think about it; if you're addicted or in bondage to something, you aren't free. Only by breaking out of it do you become free, not just physically, but mentally. "Then you will know the truth, and the truth will set you free." (John 8:32) So an addiction is not just a physical habit, but a mental one. When you control the mental, you will control the physical. The mental decision to do something always precedes physically doing it. Get your thinking right and your actions will be right.

It makes no difference if everyone else is doing it; that doesn't make it right. In fact, if everyone else is doing it, then I would say that it's more reason not to do it! Success will never be achieved by conforming to the "world." Only by doing what's right will you achieve happiness and success. Beware of who you take advice from. Don't take advice from someone just because they're your best friend. Just because they're your "best friend" doesn't mean that their advice is good or their behaviour is pleasing to God.

The Bible says, "What causes fights and quarrels

among you? Don't they come from your desires that battle within you? You want something but don't get it. You kill and covet, but you cannot have what you want. You quarrel and fight. You do not have, because you do not ask God. When you ask, you do not receive, because you ask with wrong motives, that you may spend what you get on your pleasures. You adulterous people, don't you know that friendship with the world is hatred towards God? Anyone who chooses to be a friend of the world becomes an enemy of God." (James 4:1- 4)

Although we are ultimately responsible, I would say that the TV is also largely to blame for influencing people's thinking in a negative way. Everywhere we look, we're bombarded with swear words, violence, pornography, adultery, gossip, and the like. Why not commit today to changing your habits and start reading from a positive thinking book for fifteen minutes every day? It will turn your life around. You will also begin to realise the truth about yourself by ridding yourself of false and limiting be-liefs and replacing them with the truth— the truth which has been there all the time, since the day you were born. Someone once said, that the truth is the truth, regardless of whether it's believed or not. The truth doesn't change, only our beliefs.

> "Everything is permissible for me— but not
> everything is beneficial.
> Everything is permissible for me— but I will not be
> mastered by anything."

(1 Corinthians 6:12)

for INTEGRITY

Integrity is essential if you want to become successful in life, but it's also a choice that each one of us makes. We can choose to have integrity or we can choose not to have it. In my opinion, choosing not to have integrity is doing things the hard way, because eventually things will come full circle and we will be found out. Some people are high achievers without integrity, but the only way to be truly happy and successful is when all of your dealings are for the mutual benefit of other people as well as yourself.

Some people think that money is more important than integrity, but ironically, when you have integrity, you are likely to end up making more money as a result. People are more likely to do business with you if they can trust you. The Bible says, "A good name is more desirable than great riches; to be esteemed is better than silver or gold." (Proverbs 22:1)

Winners always look for win-win situations, never win-lose situations. They're always looking for situations where there's mutual gain for themselves and the other person. Rogues look for win-lose situations, where they appear to get ahead at someone else's expense. But in reality, I don't think there really is such a thing as a win-lose situation, because while they may appear to win initially, they actually lose in the long run. So a win-lose situation, where someone thinks they are going to deceive someone for the sake of personal gain, actually turns out to be a lose-lose situation. They have, in fact, deceived themselves. "So if you think you are standing firm, be careful that you don't fall." (1 Corinthians 10:12) It simply isn't worth it to be dishonest, because in some way or another, it's going to backfire.

An extreme example of a lose-lose situation was Adolf Hitler and his Third Reich. Hitler initially thought that he was into a win-lose situation where he and his Third Reich would rule the world and everybody else would lose. But this illusion eventually turned out to be false. While he seemed to win initially, in the long run he lost. What he thought was a win-lose situation actually turned out to be a lose-lose situation. He eventually killed himself and brought total destruction to Germany and the rest of the world, costing millions of people their lives in the process. While that's an extreme example, the principle is still the same.

Lack of integrity can cause us to fail, and it can cause businesses to fail. How many times have you heard of pro-fessional football players or athletes being disqualified be-cause they tested positive for drugs and were sent home in disgrace? How many businesses have failed because of dishonest dealings which resulted in a bad reputation? How many businesses have gone out of business because they sold inferior products? We'll probably never know the answer, but it's impossible to plant negative "seeds" (dishonesty) and expect to reap positive results. Life doesn't work that way. What we give is what we get, and mother nature always seeks balance. So really, if you have no in-tegrity, the only person you're really cheating is yourself. The Bible says, "The man of integrity walks securely, but he who takes crooked paths will be found out." (Proverbs 10:9)

I remember an old friend telling me about the time they took their car to a garage. There were three different things wrong with their car, and they had been taking their car to the same garage for years. This person didn't know much about cars, and whether the garage was aware of this, I'm not sure. But anyway, the garage told them that all three things had been done, but the person had reason to doubt that everything had been done. Unknown to the garage, their father was a mechanic and checked it over. As it turned out, only two of the three things had been done. The person then quizzed the garage about it, but didn't disclose the fact that their father was a mechanic and had looked over it. The garage just simply fobbed them off with some technical jargon. So instead of causing a scene, which they could have done, they just didn't go back. Not only that, but some of their family members who were also considering using that garage decided not to. They, in turn, told their friends and acquaintances. So who knows how many potential customers that garage ended up losing, all because of one little act of dishonesty? Now I'm not saying that the person shouldn't have confronted the garage about their father looking at it; maybe they should have. But the point I want to make is this: surveys show that when people are dissatisfied with a product or service, the majority of them don't complain; they simply don't go back.

A lack of integrity can also cause us to have negative emotions which will destroy our peace of mind. Emotions such as worry, greed, guilt, and anxiety can all result from dishonesty or unethical behaviour. Remember, we cannot attract good things if our emotions are negative. Only when our emotions are positive can we attract good things, such as wealth. There might even be a difference in the quality of the customers we attract. "Do you see a man skilled in his work? He will serve before kings; he will not serve before obscure men." (Prov 22:29)

So if you want to have peace of mind and be successful, you need to practice doing what's right. Why not make it a habit to do what's right all the time and practice excellence in everything you do? If you do that, then you certainly won't have to deal with any of the negative emotions mentioned above, and you'll be a lot happier. For that reason alone it's worth it. What price do you put on peace of mind?

The way you treat other people will eventually come full circle and you'll reap a harvest based on the seeds you have sown. Only the path of integrity leads to true success and lasting happiness. It's simply a decision away. A good way to start is by simply following the golden rule: "So in everything, do to others what you would have them do to you." (Mat 7:12).

So how do you know if you have integrity or not? Well, a good test is to ask yourself what you would do if you were tempted to do something dishonest (which was going to be of great financial gain to you), but you also knew that no one else would ever find out. Would you do it or wouldn't you? If you'd resist the temptation, then you have integrity; if not, then rest assured you would suffer from greed and guilt and a poor self image. But integrity doesn't necessarily have to involve large sums of money. What we do regarding smaller things is just as important, because all the smaller things add up and they form our character. Chances are that if we're honest regarding small things, we'll also be honest when it comes to bigger things. Unfortunately, the same principle holds true for dishonesty. Just as a little test: what would you do if you bought something in a shop and the person gave you too much change? Would you give it back or would you keep it? Your answer to that determines whether you have integrity or not. If you're just as honest when no one is looking as you are when they're looking, then you have integrity.

But apart from anything else, there's such a thing as being true to yourself, and this affects your self image. Not only that, but if we're dishonest then we dishonour God. We might fool other people, or even try to fool ourselves, but we can't fool God. There's nothing in all creation that's hidden from God. "Does he who implanted the ear not hear? Does he who formed the eye not see?" (Psalm 94:9) Therefore, we really have no hiding place, even if we think we do.

Another form of integrity is being true to our word. If we say we're going to do something and we don't, then we've lost our integrity. Likewise, if we say we won't do something and do it, we've also broken our integrity. If we want to have integrity, we need to be true to our word and to adopt the attitude, "Our word is our bond." You can't effectively lead people if they can't depend on you or trust you. You'll lose credibility in their eyes and they'll stop following you. Some people think they can still lead without integrity, to which someone once replied, "Who's following you?" So if you make a commitment to do something, make sure you follow through. If you can't follow through, or have any doubts about it, say so. It's far better not to make the initial commitment than to say that you will and let them down. Guaranteed, you will lose a lot more friends by letting them down than you will by not making the initial commitment.

It's also important that we don't gossip behind people's backs. If someone shares confidential information with us, it should stay confidential and never go any further. One way to build up trust is not only by keeping our commitments, but also by keeping confidential information to ourselves. Then people will know that they can trust us and that they can also come to us with their problems in the future. Trust is a great virtue to have. It takes time to earn, but it can be lost in a second. If you're a trusted individual and respected for your integrity, I congratulate you. You will, and probably do, stand out head and shoulders above the competition. Hold on to that trust, build on it, and never let it go. Trust is one of the foundations for building good relationships. When you are trusted, whether it's in business or in personal relationships, people will be attracted to you. But remember that trust is a two-way thing. You also need to be willing to trust other people; unless of course they have already given you reason not to. So learn to trust, learn to be trusted, make your word your bond, and it will reward you.

for JOURNEY

We must remember that success is a journey, not a destination. No matter how successful we become, we never ever get to a point where we've arrived, because success is progressive and ongoing. It's not an event. Some people think that when they've achieved a certain goal, then they'll be successful. While that might be true to an extent, if we sit back after achieving the goal, then we're at the point of sliding backwards. There is no such thing as sitting still; we're either going forwards or going backwards. It stands to reason that because success is progressive and ongoing, it has to be constantly maintained by setting new goals continually. As soon as one goal is achieved we need to have another goal in place. Success is measured by what we do every day and is hidden in our daily routine.

But neither should we ever get to a point where we become complacent and stop learning or renewing our minds. Some people think that learning stops once they leave college or university, or when they've achieved their goal. But such a philosophy leads to stagnation. Some people work very hard to achieve a certain objective, such as a degree or a title, but they make the mistake of sitting back once they get there, and they stop learning. They maybe put in years of study and effort to achieve what they wanted, but as soon as they get there, they think learning is over. To them success was an event instead of being the journey itself. Now that's all very well if that's all they want out of life, but if not, then they need to make a few changes. If we reach one goal but don't have another one in place, there's an anti-climax and life can seem to have an emptiness, because one minute we're striving towards something with all our might, and the next minute we have nothing to strive towards. This is when our lives can plateau or seem to stagnate. I believe this is also one of the reasons why many people don't live long after retirement, because subconsciously they feel they don't have a purpose anymore, and life can seem meaningless and empty.

It reminds me of the true story of a man who owned a large business. One minute he was head of an empire which employed many people. He got up every day with purpose and a full schedule. He was giving orders, and people looked up to him and were very focused on accomplishing something. In other words, he was "somebody." Then when he retired, he realised he was no longer "somebody." He was no longer giving orders to anyone, and there was no one around to look up to him. Neither did he have any more goals. In fact, he felt like a "nobody." Sadly, this happens all too often when people retire. To retire is to admit to yourself subconsciously that you have reached the end of your journey. Some people claim that they're getting too old to keep working; but work doesn't necessarily have to be physical. There are many things which keep your mind active that don't require much physical effort, such as writing, painting, teaching, and public speaking, to name a few. There is really no excuse to retire unless you want to!

We, as human beings, are created to achieve and to accomplish. Our subconscious mind, by nature, is a goal-seeking mechanism. It's the way God has created us. If we suddenly deny our subconscious the dreams and goals that it craves, then it may start to work against us. Our inner self talk may change to "life is boring" or "I'll never be rich," or a host of other negative thought patterns. We may even become more pessimistic or even cynical when the subject of dreams and goals comes up.

For people who think that success is an event, their life pattern might look something like this:

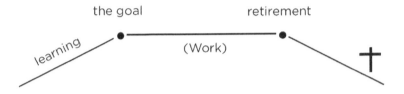

But for a person who never stops setting goals and realises that success is the journey itself, their life pattern might look more like this:

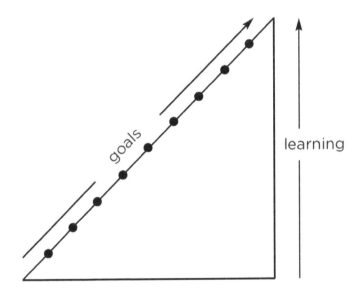

Not only do they keep setting goals for themselves, but they also continue to keep learning by controlling what goes into their minds on a daily basis. So if we want to keep achieving and make the most of our potential, the answer really is twofold: never stop setting goals and never stop learning. Then you'll never be in danger of stagnating. Apart from anything else, isn't life much more fun when you're shooting for something? And isn't life dull when you've nothing to shoot for? I remember hearing a record some time ago which was called, "The Chase Is Better Than the Catch," and I thought to myself, "There's a fair bit of truth in that," because there's always excitement in the chase. The chase is never dull, but once you get to the catch, the excitement is over because you've achieved your goal. It's when we're in the pursuit of something that we're most alive and the most alert. That's when we get the most living out of life. It's when we're stretching ourselves, facing our fears and getting out of our comfort zones that we grow mentally and feel fulfilled. That's also when we have the most energy.

I remember watching a documentary about two American veterans speaking about their experiences from the Vietnam War. Although they faced death and extreme danger every day, not only from enemy soldiers but also from booby-traps, they referred to this as "Living on the edge." Living on the edge meant that your life could be snuffed out at any second. One of them went on to say that at a time like that, "you are very much alive," because your state of mind is sharpened and your appreciation of life is much greater. But hopefully you or I won't have to go to a war zone to feel more "alive" or to sharpen all of our senses. We can do it by fighting our own financial battles back home. We can do it by setting goals and getting out of our comfort zones and facing our fears.

I once heard a motivational speaker say, "If you don't have any dreams or goals, you're dead from the neck up." Isn't it sad to see people going through life without any dreams or goals, spending a large part of their waking hours looking at a TV screen? If that's what they want then that's fine, but if not, then something has to change. In my opinion, it's not always their fault, because we're not taught to have dreams or goals. Our parents don't usually teach us, and as far as I'm aware, the school system doesn't teach it either. So how do they find out? It's up to you and me.

Why not share what you've learned with other people? Why not write a book yourself? Why not leave a legacy that will continue to inspire people long after you're gone? But whatever you do, find out what you want and at least set a goal, and then you can work on having the next goal in place. Network marketing offers people not only the unique opportunity of never running out of goals, but also the opportunity of plugging into an excellent personal development program. This, in my opinion, is more important than the money itself. Why? Because the personal development program is ultimately what will change your life by changing how you think. It will also help you to make more money in the long run. Remember, if you want your outward life to change, you must change inwardly first. That means changing how you think. Only once you have changed first will you start to see any outward changes.

But please don't misunderstand me. I'm not saying that the only way to improve your life is to get involved in a network marketing business. Not at all. What I'm saying is that, for your life to improve, you must control what goes into your mind and you must associate with positive people. Network marketing just happens to provide the environment for such opportunities. When you improve yourself mentally, it's virtually impossible for your external world not to improve, because one will always be a reflection of the other. It's really a case of "get yourself right and your world will be right." Many people want to improve their lives but are unwilling to improve themselves. This, in my opinion, is why so many people fail, or live lives of mediocrity at best.

They make the mistake of seeking happiness externally while refusing to change their habits and their thinking. As a result, their journey of life never improves, and it continues to be one of frustration and failure. They may have the occasional "high point," but it's usually short lived before they slide back into the rut of daily living. They fail to realise that as you improve, so does your journey. It's impossible to change one without changing the other. The quality of your life will always be in direct proportion to the quality of your inner world. If there is turmoil inside, there will be turmoil outside. If there is peace, beauty, and riches inside, there will be peace, beauty, and riches outside.

I'm reminded of the story of a little boy who kept pestering his father to play games with him. His dad was trying to relax after a hard day's work and couldn't be bothered, so he kept giving his son one toy after another, in the hope that he would leave him alone. But he kept coming back. So finally his dad had an idea; there was a great big map of the world, and what he did was rip it up into loads of little pieces, gave it to his son, and said, "There, son. Put that back together for me." Dad thought, "That should keep him busy for at least an hour or two." But to his utter amazement, within about ten minutes his son had successfully stuck it all back together and said, "Look, Dad, I've finished it!" His dad wondered how on earth he could have finished it so quickly and so successfully, and he said, "How did you manage to do that?"And the little boy said, "Well you see, Dad, on the back of the picture of the world, there's a picture of a man, and all I done was put the man back together. I figured that when the man's right, the world will be right."

Doesn't that tell us something? Maybe we need to concentrate less on what's external and concentrate more on what's internal. Then the external will take care of itself, and everything else will fall into place. Of course, we still need to have dreams and goals, because they are vitally important to our success, but they should never be at the expense of self improvement. It's impossible to improve yourself without having your external world improve accordingly. When we improve, our journey improves automatically.

REMEMBER TO STOP AND SMELL THE ROSES

We must remember that our journey of life isn't just about work. Part of the journey is taking the time to appreciate magic moments, because once they're gone, they're gone forever. I remember one summer morning I woke up in the early hours just before sunrise. It was broad daylight even although it was only about 4:00 a.m. I looked out my bedroom window across the deep blue sea, which looked like glass. The blue sky reflected in the calm water as the horizon became a sort of reddish orange colour. I knew the sun was about to rise any minute. I knew it was going to be a beautiful day. There was no noise except for the birds and the occasional vehicle. I had gotten up to use the bathroom and was tempted to go right back to bed, but something told me to wait and watch the sunrise. Suddenly, the first ray of light came through the window. How beautiful and how peaceful, I thought! I'm so glad I stayed up a few more minutes to see such a beautiful sight. I went back to bed and slept like a log.

for KNOWLEDGE

Do you know what can expand while staying the same size? The answer is our minds. When we learn and increase our knowledge, we expand our minds. Although our brains take up a certain amount of space, our capacity to learn and retain information is unlimited. Some people place limits on themselves unnecessarily by saying things such as, "I've got a terrible memory" or "I could never learn all that." Not only is this false, but it also demeans the "equipment" God has given us. There is nothing wrong with our "equipment;" the problem lies in our own limiting beliefs and negative self talk. As Henry Ford wisely put it, "You can if you think you can, but if you think you can't, you're right too."

The truth is that you can learn whatever you have the desire to learn, if you are willing to pay the price. Why choose to have self-imposed limitations if you were not born with any? What a foolish way to live life! You also have a perfect memory, but you may not believe that. Some people have conditioned themselves to forget things by saying, "I've got a terrible memory." It's not that there's anything wrong with their memory, but they've programmed their subconscious to forget by the words they speak. You can limit the effectiveness of something by giving it faulty in-structions, or you can use it to its full potential by giving it the right instructions. There's no limit to what you can learn if you have a strong enough desire to learn it.

So how do we increase our knowledge? We do it by reading positive mental attitude books, listening to motivational and educational CDs, and by listening to people who are more successful than we are. Now that is all very well for increasing our knowledge, but to become valuable it has to be put into practice. Knowledge, when applied, leads to wisdom, and can improve our lives in so many ways. Knowledge of people skills can improve our relationships with other people and it can also improve our financial situation. Knowledge of how our minds work can make us happier and more successful. Knowledge can enable us to deal successfully with situations that we might otherwise not have been able to cope with. Knowledge of God's word, in the eyes of a Christian, is the ultimate kind of knowledge. I can honestly say from my own point of view that if I had known years ago some of the words of wisdom in the Bible, I could have saved myself from falling into many pitfalls, and saved myself from years of pain and hardship. Because of a lack of knowledge, I took many foolish paths. The Bible says, "My people are destroyed from a lack of knowledge." (Hosea 4:6) Also, in the book of Proverbs it says, "Choose my instruction instead of silver, knowledge rather than choice gold, for wisdom is more precious than rubies, and nothing you desire can compare with her." (Prov 8:10-11)

I often wonder why this isn't taught in schools. Even in high school we're often taught to read some kind of fictional book, which will do nothing for us in the real world, rather than read something that will teach us wisdom and rock solid principles, which will stand us in good stead in life. As far as I'm aware, the school system teaches little or nothing about having a positive mental attitude or saving ten percent of your income. It doesn't teach anything about reaping what you sow, or that creating your own destiny is determined by how you think. And it teaches little or nothing about business ownership or financial intelligence. Don't get me wrong, I know that we're taught a lot of valuable things in school, such as reading and writing and other diverse subjects, and I am sure that a lot of teachers are good at what they do, but why are the most important things left out? I don't know. Therefore, it's up to us educate ourselves. We need to realise that there are different kinds of intelligences. Most of the teaching in the school system is geared towards getting a job, and people are not really encouraged to think outside "the box."

For example, there's a difference between academic intelligence and financial intelligence, or academic intelligence and emotional intelligence, or academic intelligence and relational intelligence. These are all different types of intelligences. Just because a person is intelligent in one area doesn't mean they're automatically intelligent in another. In fact, some people are highly intelligent in one area and very unintelligent in other areas. For example, a person might be highly educated academically but do foolish things with their money. Or they might be highly educated but have poor relations with other people. Or they might be highly educated but lack emotional control. All of these things can, and usually do, lead to failure. And all of these things can be traced to a lack of knowledge. So if we want to be truly successful, we must work on increasing our knowledge in all areas instead of just one.

Another way of increasing our knowledge is by associating with and seeking advice from people who are more successful than we are. In other words, have a mentor who has a genuine interest in you and who you can trust. Don't just take someone's advice simply because they're your friend or because you've known them for a long time. That has nothing to do with it. For example, suppose you wanted advice on a "million dollar" business idea. Your best friend might never have made anywhere near a million dollars in their life, or ever been in business, yet you might be tempted to listen to them and take their advice. How can they possibly give you good financial advice if they haven't achieved themselves? If they had good financial advice, don't you think they would already have achieved it? The only way to get good financial advice is when the person has, firstly, already achieved in that area and secondly, they must have your interest at heart.

Seek an opportunity where the person you're seeking advice from has their success built on your success. If they gave you faulty advice, they would be hurting their own business. In other words, it has to be a win-win situation.

Sadly, today there are very few people who have your interest at heart, let alone who give you good advice. The Bible says, "Gold there is, and rubies in abundance, but lips that speak knowledge are a rare jewel." (Proverbs 20:15).

Our ability to remember things also plays an important part in making full use of our knowledge. If you have a hard time remembering things, it could be because you've told yourself for such a long time that you have a terrible memory, and your subconscious mind has been faithfully responding by making sure that you do have a terrible memory. Remember that you program your subconscious to succeed or fail by the words you speak. Why not start saying things like, "My memory is improving every day;" then you'll be programming yourself for success instead of failure.

Another reason that you might not remember things could be because you're under stress. Sometimes, when we're under stress, we don't try hard enough to remember it in the first place. Sometimes we have too much on our minds and we don't concentrate. This is no fault of our memory, because in order to remember, we first have to make a vivid impression by consciously taking it in. In other words, to vividly recall, we have to vividly impress. If we don't take it in properly, or we aren't concentrating, then we won't be able to remember it. As a result, some people start to blame their memory and start saying they've got a terrible memory, thus programming themselves to fail. This only results in creating a vicious circle which reinforces their limiting beliefs. The truth is, there is no limit to what you can remember— unless you choose to limit yourself by negative words!

Stress and negative emotions cloud your memory and stop it from functioning as well as it should. I've seen myself in situations where I point blank could not recall a car registration or phone number which I knew off by heart, all because I was stressed! I knew that I knew it, but could not recall it. Only when my emotional state returned to positive was I able to effortlessly recall the number, which had been in my subconscious all the time. The problem with stress is that it creates a block between the conscious and subconscious. Although all the information is stored in the subconscious, we need to be able to consciously remember (or withdraw) information from the storehouse of the subconscious when necessary. When our emotional state is positive, communication between our conscious and subconscious parts of the mind are in perfect harmony.

Any habit, behaviour, or action which causes negative emotions will tend to dominate your mind and cloud your memory. This could include watching TV, listening to the radio, or reading negative literature such as a newspaper, or even something pornographic. Most people saturate their minds with negativity day in and day out. Remember what we said earlier about emotions being far more powerful than our conscious thoughts? Emotions, whether positive or negative, will always dominate our thinking. When our emotions are positive we can think clearly, but when they're negative we don't think clearly. We also have less energy.

If we want to improve our memory as well as increasing our knowledge, we need to avoid negative sources of input such as TV, radio, and newspapers, and concentrate instead on positive books, motivational CDs, and uplifting music. Believe it or not, there is such a thing as positive and negative music. So how do we know if music is positive or negative? Well, a good guide is to check your emotions. For example, if a certain type of music caused you to feel aggressive, then that could be classed as negative music. Or if it caused you to feel self pity, that could also be classed as negative music. But positive music will uplift you and make you think happy thoughts. The lyrics to a piece of music are also important. Sometimes we don't even consider what the words are. Sometimes they are downright negative; other times they are positive.

So what has memory got to do with knowledge? Quite a lot actually, because what use is knowledge if you can't remember it? For knowledge to be useful it first has to be remembered. So it makes sense to work on improving our memory. Many books have been written on the subject of memory, but from what I've learned (or remembered), the most effective way of remembering something is to first of all create a vivid mental picture of it, and secondly, make it as ridiculous as possible. Why? Because firstly, we don't think in words or numerals, we think in pictures. And secondly, the more ridiculous something is, the more likely it is to be remembered. For example, if you wanted to remember to take something with you, such as a cheque book, instead of just saying, "I must remember to take my cheque book," why not create a vivid mental picture of a cheque book and make it as ridiculous as possible? For example, you might picture a bright orange check-book which is so big that it cannot fit in your house. And then replay that image over and over in your mind until it is cemented in. The more detail you can include, the better. You might even picture some of your friends outside in the garden holding it up because it's so big. You could even picture it being so big that it's taking up the whole length of the street and is taller than the lamp-posts. Then you'll have no problem remembering it because it's so ridiculous. Ridiculous things tend to stick in our minds, but ordinary things are easily forgotten. Such techniques can be a valuable aid in situations such as sitting exams, or even just day to day living. The more you exercise your memory, the easier it will become to remember. It's like keeping fit mentally.

Another technique for remembering is by means of

association. By that I mean associating something with what we need to remember. For example, if you wanted to remember numerals such as a phone number, you might want to break the numbers down into pairs of numbers (if the number is quite long) and then associate each pair of numbers with something, such as a particular year. For example, if you wanted to remember the number 663245, you might associate 66 with a certain event in 1966. The number 32 you might associate with a person's age or waist size (if appropriate), and the number 45 you might associate with the year the Second World War ended. But you decide on the connection that's easiest for you to remember; then concentrate on remembering the events, rather than the numerals. Being able to recall events is easier than simply remembering numbers, because we think in pictures, and pictures make a far bigger impression on our subconscious mind. Being able to remember things, such as important details and people's names, will stand us in good stead in our relations with other people, and it can also help us in business. In fact, being able to remember will help us in every aspect of our lives.

for LEARN

Wouldn't you agree that our entire life is a learning process? It doesn't matter how educated we are or how many degrees we have, we are always learning something and life is always teaching us lessons. In fact, sometimes being highly educated can be a handicap if it leads to an attitude of complacency and close-mindedness to learning more. We should always keep an open mind, no matter how much we know. This is part of becoming wise. We may disagree with what we are being told, but we should be open-mindeed enough to consider what is being said before discarding it. We should always be hungry to learn and we should always have the attitude that we're never going to know enough. This reminds me of the story of the highly educated, highly paid professional who joined a multi-level marketing business. The person who sponsored him into the business was much younger than him, probably about half his age, but he had a lot of experience in the business.

The younger person, who we will call "Joe," knew that in order to succeed in the business it was essential to be attending seminars and reading positive books. He also knew the value of having an up-line mentor in the business, and he knew how important it was to listen to their advice. Joe knew that the only people who had ever achieved a great deal of success were the ones who got plugged into the system and followed the recommended pattern. He had seen many people join the business and many people leave. Most of the ones who left never ever got committed to the system. Many of them were unteachable and thought they could build the business without the system. The problem was that the highly educated professional, who we will call Mr. Smith, was not open minded to Joe's advice. He thought that, because he was successful in his own profession, he would automatically be successful in this business. He thought that his skills and expertise would somehow carry over and that he wouldn't need the system. He was wrong. To add to the problem, he also thought that no one who was so much younger than him could ever teach him anything. Wrong again. Through a lack of knowledge, he didn't realise that this kind of business levels the playing field. This meant that it didn't matter what a person had achieved outside this business; it was irrelevant. This was different. It required different training, a different way of thinking, different skills, and a different mindset.

The problem with Mr. Smith, and for many other people coming into this kind of business, is that they come in with an "employee mindset" and don't realise that you need to develop "business ownership mentality" in order to succeed. Different skills are required, such as skill at dealing with people and learning to speak in public, as well as practicing delayed gratification. If you already have your own full-time business and are used to dealing with or even employing people, you might be tempted to think that you don't need the system either. Wrong. Everybody needs the system. We need it not only for education but also for motivation.

If we fail to put positivity into our minds every day, we will eventually be defeated by our own negative thinking. Most people don't realise this unless they're willing to learn. In the case of Mr. Smith, he also didn't realise that a person's age made absolutely no difference as to how experienced or successful they were. He thought that age and seniority automatically equated with success. Wrong again, Mr. Smith. As you probably guessed, Mr. Smith didn't last long in the business, because he wasn't willing to learn. He could have become successful in the business if he was willing to change his attitude and learn. He had the potential, but his mind was closed. As a result of his unwillingness to learn, he limited his future in terms of what he could achieve. Don't let that happen to you. It might not be a multi-level marketing business you get involved in, but don't let an unwillingness to learn become an obstacle to your future. Take the limits off and take the barriers down. Welcome the chance to learn. Look upon it as an opportunity to increase your knowledge, rather than as a burden to bear.

LEARNING FROM MISTAKES

One of the best ways to learn something is to learn from our mistakes. When we make a mistake, we learn what doesn't work and we learn not to repeat it or it will lead to failure. These 'mistakes' should actually be viewed as valuable learning experiences rather than viewed in a negative light. Some people are extremely critical of other people for making mistakes, and they say things like, "It should never have happened," or "You should have known better!" This is an extremely negative attitude to take because it is impossible to succeed in anything without making mistakes. If we don't make mistakes then how are we going to learn? How will we gain experience? How will we know which roads to take and which ones to avoid?

It's only by doing something and going through the process of trial and error that we gain experience. And it's only through experience that we truly learn. People need to be allowed the freedom to fail. If you don't allow them the freedom to fail, not only will they resent you, but they will develop a "fear" of failing. People do not perform well when they're operating in a mindset of fear. All creative thinking is then stifled because fear is dominating their thinking instead. Remember what we said earlier about the danger of negative emotions? Therefore, to rid them of fear and maximise their performance, they need to know that you're not going to jump all over them every time they make a mistake. Instead you should be more concerned about the lesson they learned from that mistake, possibly giving them some encouragement, and telling them that you have faith in them that they won't make the same mistake again.

When it comes to learning, we can learn a certain amount by reading or listening, but that alone isn't enough. We only truly learn by actually "doing." Each mistake or "temporary defeat" is actually a pointer, pointing us in another direction. The more times we fail, the more pointers we have, and the clearer the road to success becomes. If you are failing a lot, you are learning a lot. But we also need to be taking corrective action and not making the same mistakes over and over. This will lead to wisdom and ultimately success.

That's what winners do. They turn failure into success by taking corrective action. They analyse each defeat, find out what didn't work, and use it as a pointer towards corrective action. As painful as each defeat might have been, they still view it positively by using it as a learning experience, so that even in the worst of failures there's something to be learned from it. For example, someone might invest a lot of money in something and end up losing the whole lot. The average person will focus on the money lost, but the successful person will focus on the lessons learned from the experience. They will analyse their defeat, find out where they went wrong, and determine never to make the same mistake again.

Someone once said that the height of insanity is to keep doing the same thing over and over, expecting different results. Something has to change if we want the results to change. But sometimes we might be unsure of which road to take, and we have to risk failing again in order to find out. Well, I can only speak from my own experience and what has helped me, but each time that I've asked God for guidance, things have always in the end worked out for my highest good. I say "in the end" because often there were more failures ahead and more mistakes to be made. But these often painful experiences turned out to be nuggets of wisdom that I could not have succeeded without.

The Bible also gives us some support here: "I will instruct you and teach you in the way you should go; I will counsel you and watch over you." (Psalm 32:8) And in the book of Proverbs we are told, "Trust in the Lord with all your heart and lean not on your own understanding; in all your ways acknowledge Him and He will make your paths straight." (Prov 3:5-6) These verses have been of great comfort to me because I know that no matter how badly I've messed up, this too is part of Gods plan for my life and He is ultimately in control. The truth is that we are always taking one of two roads: one that leads to success or one that is going to teach us a valuable lesson. If you can learn to view things in that way, then even failure can be viewed in a positive light.

But learning from mistakes doesn't always have to be from our own mistakes. If we are wise, we can also learn from other people's mistakes. For example, I've seen people buy property, and while it seemed like a good move initially, as time went by it became apparent that what seemed like a good location was actually a bad location. It turned out that it was much busier and far noisier than expected because of where it was situated, but neither of these things was apparent when they bought it. Although I felt genuinely sorry for them, I also realised that I myself would avoid a similar location. It has often been said that when you're buying property you should view it morning, noon, and night, because what might seem like a quiet location during the day can seem like an entirely different place in the evening. So if someone else has already made the mistake, learn from it.

In war, military commanders have to use failure as a learning device in order to keep one step ahead of the enemy. In World War II, crews from American B-17 bombers (nicknamed Flying Fortresses) flying deep into Germany suffered appalling losses at the hands of single-engine Nazi fighters. The U.S. Air chiefs believed that because of the defensive firepower of the B-17, which was eleven machine guns (initially), this would be enough to beat off the German fighters without too many losses. They were about to find out otherwise, just as the British had already found out. The Royal Air Force had already switched to bombing at night because of the heavy losses sustained during daylight raids. The Luftwaffe ruled the skies over Germany. The problem the Americans faced was that because they specialised in "precision bombing," which meant bombing specific targets rather than a whole city, they needed to fly during daylight for accuracy. The other problem was that our fighter escorts lacked the range to go all the way to the target and back, and could only escort the bombers so far. So General Curtis Lemay introduced a new formation called the "combat box." This meant that the bombers were stacked and staggered in such a way that each bomber in the group was covered by the guns of every other one. This now provided concentrated firepower for a thousand yards in every direction. But the losses were still heavy. According to some of the crews, they still didn't have enough machine guns, even although they had the famous 'Flying Fort.'

But as time went on, the Germans were learning, too. They learned to go for the leader and try to split up the formation. They also learned that if they attacked the formation head on, the top turret on the B-17 couldn't come down below level and the ball turret underneath couldn't fire up. So the front was open. Once again, the German fighters exploited this weakness and took a terrible toll on the bombers. So the U.S. Eighth Air Force responded by adding an extra turret under the chin of the B-17, but this was still not enough. Finally a breakthrough was made. The breakthrough was to add extra fuel tanks under the wings of a brand new fighter, the P-51 Mustang. This fighter, which now had the range of a bomber, was able to accompany the bombers all the way to the target and back. The German fighters, which once were hunters of the American bombers, were now the "hunted" of the American fighters. Subsequent missions now saw the tide starting to turn against the Germans. Some German fighters still got through and some bombers were still lost, but where the Mustangs were present, it was the Luftwaffe that got shot out of the sky.

Gradually the Allies gained air superiority over the enemy's homeland, which led to the ultimate defeat of Nazi Germany. But one of the reasons the Allied Forces won the war was because they kept learning from their defeats and taking corrective action. What would have happened if our military strategists had let temporary defeat stop them? What would have happened if they had failed to learn from their defeats? We would have lost the war, just as some people in business allow temporary defeat to stop them and lose sight of their dreams. Once again, the learning process holds true, whether in war or business:

for MONEY

What is your opinion of money? Now that's a question that usually evokes a variety of different responses from people, because people sometimes have vastly different beliefs about money. Some people believe it's good to be rich while others believe that it's wrong to be rich. Some people believe in free enterprise and the Capitalist system while others believe in Socialism. Some people believe that the best way to help someone is by giving them a hand up, and helping them to help themselves. Others believe in giving handouts. But whatever your beliefs are, understand that this will be manifested in your physical world. For example, if you believed that it was wrong to be rich, you will probably struggle financially for the rest of your life. Subconsciously you will repel money. If a person who believed it was wrong to be rich suddenly came into money unexpectedly, they may even feel guilty for having it. This sometimes happens when a person inherits money or wins the lottery. The emotion of guilt can cause them to do foolish things subconsciously, causing them to get rid of the money. Needless to say that they lose it pretty quickly or run into major problems. Whereas someone who believed it was good to be rich would attract wealth, and would attract opportunities for creating wealth. Either way, our beliefs will eventually manifest themselves physically.

If you want to see in an improvement in your financial situation, there has to be a change mentally, and also in your habits. Most people don't change their attitude towards money. Neither do they change their habits, yet they still hope to see changes externally. This is usually a recipe for failure and frustration. So what internal changes do we need to make? Well, first of all, we need to change our thinking. If you want to become wealthy, you need to recognise that money is good and not evil. It's true that some people do evil things for money, but money itself is not evil. It's people who are evil because of their attitude toward money. Only when you believe that money is good will you begin to attract it. Only then will you begin to adopt the necessary wealth habits such as saving, tithing, and investing. Part of investing is being willing to invest in ourselves by committing to our ongoing education and personal development. Most people don't do that. Instead, most people read newspapers, watch TV, use the same old negative words such as "I can't afford it," and wonder why nothing improves externally. The reason nothing improves externally is because they contribute to their own misery. Some people save nothing, invest nothing, give nothing, and get themselves into debt. That is financial suicide!

As in anything, there are failure habits and success habits; money is no different. Most people would like to have more money but are unwilling to do anything about it. Some people will turn down every opportunity that comes their way because of fear of getting out of their comfort zone. Unfortunately, we cannot do anything for these people, but we can help people who are willing to get out of their comfort zones and help themselves. I believe God helps those who help themselves, but I also believe He helps those who help other people. Part of financial success is being willing to give away a tenth of your income to people less fortunate than yourself. The Bible refers to this as "tithing," meaning to give a tenth. Believe it or not, this will be at the very centre of your financial wellbeing, and your financial situation will improve a hundredfold. This is a major success habit, but if ignored, it will lead to failure. Greed and selfishness are major failure habits which lead to poverty. To the extent you give will be to the extent that you receive, and more. In the Bible we're reminded of the benefits of tithing. "'Bring the whole tithe into the store-house, that there may be food in my house. Test me in this,' says the Lord Almighty 'and see if I will not throw open the floodgates of heaven, and pour out so much blessing that you will not have room enough for it. I will prevent pests from devouring your crops, and the vines in your fields will not cast their fruit,' says the Lord Almighty. 'Then all the nations will call you blessed, for yours will be a delightful land,' says the Lord Almighty." (Malachi 3:10-12)

Another thing that you might need to change is your spending habits. Some people have interest working for them and some people have interest working against them. Some people save a portion of what they earn, and some people save nothing. In fact, some people do even worse than that and get themselves into serious debt.

Remember that interest is neutral and can either give you a source of passive income or it can destroy your finances. Which do you prefer? Why not cut up the credit cards today? Why not decide that unless you can afford to pay cash for something, you will do without? I must admit that this was a hard step for me initially, but what happens is, when you develop new, positive financial habits, such as giving and saving, your financial situation improves anyway. In his book, The Richest Man in Babylon, George S. Clason recommends saving ten percent of your income. This is a habit that is well worth developing and will serve you well. Who knows when you might need extra cash for an emergency? Saving also teaches you discipline. As you begin to see your savings grow, eventually you start getting paid interest on the interest and it grows exponentially.

If you are in debt you might want to allocate fifty percent of what you would normally save towards getting out of debt. That way you can still continue to build your "nest egg" while the other fifty percent goes towards getting rid of the "killer interest." Some financial gurus will tell you to get rid of "all debt" before starting to save, but from what I've learned, many people who adopt that policy get discouraged and never ever start saving. They get disheartened because they see no progress in terms of savings. There always has to be something in it for yourself, or else you will get discouraged.

Another mistake people make is they go into debt for luxuries. They might see an advertisement on TV or in a magazine and get sucked in by smooth-talking sales reps who make the monthly payments sound so easy. They may be tempted by slogans such as "pay nothing for a year" or "interest free for six months!" The problem here is short term thinking. The people who get sucked in by these deals tend not to think about the next few years and what the interest rates will be then. They might forget that they're already in debt and have interest working against them. This can be an emotional battle as well as a logical one, because when you see something really appealing, not only does it appeal to your emotion of desire, but you might be pressured into buying it by your "friends." Sometimes the advertising companies use celebrities or well known TV personalities to encourage people to buy things, all of which can cause people to go into debt. Younger people are especially vulnerable to this because a lot of younger people have "role models" or "heroes" and are more likely to take their advice. Robert Kiyosaki explains in his books (The Rich Dad series) that there is good debt and bad debt. Good debt is when you are making more money because of the debt. For example, if you have purchased a rental property and you have a mortgage on it, but it's providing you with a rental income which is greater than the total expenditure, that is classed as good debt because it's providing you with a positive cash flow.

Bad debt is debt which costs you money and causes a negative cash flow, such as getting into credit card debt. For example, if you have a mortgage on the house you're living in, although it may be a necessity, it is still classed as bad debt because there is no income, only expenditure, therefore it drains your finances. Whereas the same house, if rented out, could become an asset if the rental income were to exceed the mortgage and all other expenditures. Each situation is different and unique.

Obviously there may be times when you need to go into debt for things such as buying a house, but the point I am making is this: if you want to improve your financial situation, never go into debt for a luxury. Either save for it or do without. Personally, I don't ever go into debt for a car, even though it is a necessity. Although a car may be a necessity, it's not an asset. A car will never go up in value; it will always depreciate, while you still have the same expenses. An asset is something which increases your income, and therefore a car is classed as a liability because it only costs you money. Whereas if that same car was used as a taxi and brought in more income than all the total expenditures, it would become an asset.

I once heard a guy say that one of the most selfish things he had ever heard was when someone said, "I don't want to be rich; I just want enough to get by." And the reason he said it was selfish was because, if that's their mentality, then who are they thinking of? Only themselves. Obviously there is no crime in not wanting to be rich, but someone who says "I just want enough to get by" usually has little thought for anyone else. Their thinking is flawed because they're assuming that being rich means keeping it all to yourself rather than glorifying God by using it for the benefit of mankind.

Remember, God still wants you to enjoy your life, too. He only asks us for a tenth, therefore if someone was to become rich and give away twenty, thirty or even forty percent of their income, is it wrong to be rich? I don't think so! How many people do you know who are able to give that amount away? And I don't mean to the government. Understand that broke people can't do that because they don't have the choice. Money is power. It gives us the power to do things that we otherwise couldn't do. God won't judge us on the actual amount given; He will judge us on the percentage given. Therefore, it is possible for someone who is extremely poor to be giving more than someone who is rich, because it's a percentage. And that is exactly how God views it. But having money or not having money has nothing to do with whether you are a good or a bad person. There are good and bad on both sides. Loving money is what makes you bad. There are rich people who love money and there are poor people who love money. There are kind rich people and there are kind poor people. The Bible does not condemn money itself, it condemns loving money. "For the love of money is a root of all kinds of evil." (1 Tim 6:10)

Some people who are critical of the rich say things like, "That's ridiculous, he doesn't deserve all that," without knowing what they're doing with the money. You don't know what someone else is doing with their money, whether they're rich, middle class, or poor, so no one has the right to criticise anyone. No one has the right to assume and no one has the right to judge except God Almighty. The Bible gives many warnings to the rich, not because it is wrong to be rich, but because of the dangers associated with being rich. For example, we are told, "People who want to get rich fall into temptation and a trap and into many foolish and harmful desires that plunge men into ruin and destruction." (1 Tim 6:9) But you don't have to be one of them!

Whereas we are also told in the Bible, "With me are riches and honour, enduring wealth and prosperity." (Prov 8:18).

"Bestowing wealth on those who love me and making their treasuries full." (Prov 8: 21) And if it was wrong to be rich, why does God say "Prosperity after turning to the Lord" in Deuteronomy 30? We need to remember that poverty is a curse for disobedience and prosperity is a reward for obedience. (See Lev 26 and Deut 28.) Is it any coincidence that the wealthiest countries in the world are Christian countries? I don't think so. If we obey Him we will be richly blessed, but if we disobey Him, then we will have to suffer the consequences. The best way to help someone is by helping them to help themselves. Capitalism is a system of helping people to help themselves so that they can become independent. The old saying is very true: "Give a man a fish and you feed him for a day, but teach a man to fish and he can feed himself for a lifetime." Capitalism is a system of teaching people to fish. Socialism is a system of giving people fish. The problem is that when you give people fish, you will have to feed them forever. You will not create wealthy entrepreneurs by giving people fish. Only by teaching them to fish will you encourage them to become independent instead of dependent.

Finally, for the benefit of anyone who just wants enough to get by, I'd like to share the parable of the talents. I also believe that this makes it clear that God wants us to increase our wealth, and that Capitalism, not Socialism is what honors God. "Again, it will be like a man going on a journey, who called his servants and entrusted his property to them. To one he gave five talents of money, to another two talents, and to another one talent, each according to his ability. Then he went on his journey. The man who had received the five talents went at once and put his money to work and gained five more. So also, the one with the two talents gained two more. But the man who had received the one talent went off, dug a hole in the ground and hid his master's money.

"After a long time, the master of those servants returned and settled accounts with them. The man who had received the five talents brought the other five. 'Master,' he said, 'you entrusted me with five talents. See, I have gained five more.' His master replied, 'Well done, good and faithful servant! You have been faithful with a few things; I will put you in charge of many things. Come and share your master's happiness!' The man with the two talents also came. 'Master,' he said, 'you entrusted me with two talents; see, I have gained two more.' His master replied, 'Well done good and faithful servant! You have been faithful with a few things; I will put you in charge of many things. Come and share your master's happiness!' Then the man who received the one talent came. 'Master,' he said, 'I knew that you are a hard man, harvesting where you have not sown and gathering where you have not scattered seed. So I was afraid and went out and hid your talent in the ground. See, here is what belongs to you.'

"His master replied, 'You wicked, lazy servant! So you knew that I harvest where I have not sown and gather where I have not scattered seed? Well then, you should have put my money on deposit with the bankers, so that when I returned I would have received it back with interest.

"Take the talent from him and give it to the one who has the ten talents. For everyone who has will be given more, and he will have an abundance. Whoever does not have, even what he has will be taken from him. And throw that worthless servant outside, into the darkness, where there will be weeping and gnashing of teeth.'" (Mat 25:14-30).

for NO!

Sometimes in life we need to say no to some things that are going to hold us back or take us further away from our dreams. Knowing when to say no and having the courage to say it is the sign of a leader. Sometimes we have to say no because we simply cannot do what we are being asked to do and have to politely refuse. It could be that we are too busy or we may feel that what we are being asked to do could either compromise our values or sidetrack us from our true purpose in life. Some people think that if they never refuse anyone then they will be more popular and well liked. Actually, the opposite is true. The inability to say no is actually a weakness of character and is usually rooted in the emotion of fear. The person who cannot say no is usually a "people pleaser" and would rather waste people's time and give them the run around than simply tell them no in the first place. They are afraid that if they say no they will be disliked and become unpopular. Often their whole life is a popularity contest, trying to be everything to everybody. But as we all know, this is futile, because no matter how hard we try, it is impossible to please everybody. People will have more respect for you if you tell them you're not interested, rather than pretending you are but are afraid to say no. It reminds me of the story of the person who was shown a business opportunity which had the potential to make a lot of extra money. The person who got shown the opportunity we shall call Mr. Jones, and the person who showed him the opportunity we shall call Mike.

One day Mike was talking to Mr. Jones, and in the course of conversation Mike told him he was expanding a business. Mike asked him if he was interested in looking at a business idea.

Mr. Jones replied "Of course; I'm always interested in looking at ideas."

Mike said, "Great! I've got Tuesday or Thursday evening free. Which suits you best?"

Mr. Jones: "How about Tuesday at 8:00 p.m.?"

Mike: "That's fine with me. I'll put that in my diary right now and I'll arrange to pop round and show you the idea. I'll be coming straight from work, which is about a two hour drive, so I should make it for 8:00 p.m. alright."

Mr. Jones: "Okay, see you then."

On Tuesday Mike made his way straight from work, battling rush hour traffic in order to get there for 8:00 p.m. He didn't have time to have a meal, so he had a snack on the way. When he got there, he showed Mr. Jones the presentation, which took about an hour. At the end of the presentation he asked Mr. Jones what his level of interest was. The choices were:

(1) Interested, ready to get started
(2) Need more information
(3) Not interested.

Mr. Jones said, "That looks really good! I'm interested and ready to get started."

Mike said, "Great! I'll leave you these materials explaining the next step, and I'll come back on Thursday to help you get started." So Mike left and continued on his two hour drive back home, thinking, "Great! Things are looking good!" On Thursday Mike arrived back at the house for 8:00 p.m. as arranged, but there was no answer. Then he noticed a note on the door saying, "Sorry, couldn't make it. Phone me." He also noticed his materials in a plastic bag next to the door. So he took his materials and drove back home. The next day Mike tried phoning him but couldn't get a hold of him because his line was busy. After another couple of days Mike finally managed to speak to him and asked him if he was still interested.

Mr. Jones said, "Yes I am, but I've got someone with me right now, can you phone me next week and we'll arrange something?"

So Mike said, "Okay, speak to you next week," and hung up the phone.

When next week came, Mike tried calling him but had problems getting a hold of him again. Finally, after about a week, Mike managed to speak to him to find out what the situation was.

Mr. Jones replied, "I'm really sorry I've been difficult to get a hold of, but things are really hectic at work just now. To be honest, I think it's a great idea but it's really not a good time for me to be considering other options at the moment. Sorry if I've wasted your time."

"No problem," Mike said and hung up the phone.

The truth was that Mr. Jones knew all along that he had no intention of getting involved in anything else, but he didn't want to offend Mike by saying no. Now what do you think Mike would have preferred? Being told no in the first place or going through all that? What would you prefer? Being told no or having your time and effort wasted? Mr. Jones thought Mike would have been offended if he had told him no, but the truth is that Mike loves to hear the word "no" because then he knows where he stands and he can spend his valuable time and energy elsewhere. Obviously Mike also loves to hear the word "yes" if it is a genuine yes. Genuine "yeses" and genuine "no's," Mike loves them both. What he doesn't like are wishy-washy answers and people wasting his time.

Now that is just an example, but how often do things

like that happen in everyday life? Unfortunately, quite a lot. People who are afraid to say "no" because they fear becoming unpopular actually end up becoming unpopular! They attract the very thing they fear. It's a psychological principle that if you allow fear to control your actions, you attract what you fear. In this case, fear of being unpopular caused Mr. Jones to become unpopular. But if he had refused to listen to his fear and simply said no in the first place, he would have been more respected and highly thought of. He would also have felt better about himself. This might sound ironic, but you've got to get over the fear of what people think, especially if you want to be popular. Sometimes making a stand, regardless of what people think, can cause you to be admired and respected. People who feel they can't say 'no' are often perceived as wishy-washy and weak.

Saying no can also mean self sacrifice when we are pursuing our dreams. Sometimes we need to practice "delayed gratification" and temporarily say no to some things just now, such as playing sports, clubbing, or watching TV, so that we can spend even more time doing them later on. If we don't say no just now, then these things will become an obstacle to our dreams. You may be a member of a club and have to put it on hold until you achieve your dreams. You might love to play golf but have to cut down the amount of times you play so that later on you can afford to own a golf course. Remember, winners always think long term. You may also find that a lot of your friends and colleagues are not as ambitious as you. They may start to criticise you or ridicule you for pursuing your dreams.

They may try to pull you back down to their level of ambition, which is no ambition at all! Therefore, you might have to say no to associating with them if you want to achieve your dreams. These so called "friends" can often turn out to be dream stealers if you keep hanging around with them. Often this leads to a fork in the road, where you are forced to choose between your dreams and your "friends." They may say things like, "Come on, what's wrong with you? You've been acting kind of weird since you got involved in that business. Come with us, you'll have a much better time!" And sometimes it's not easy to say no when you're under pressure from your friends. But remember, they're not going to help you become wealthy or walk on the beaches of the world. They're not going to pay off your mortgage or pay for your children's education, so why should you listen to them? Don't be afraid to say no!

Sometimes we need to say no because a person is a bad influence on us. Maybe they are deceitful or dishonest and are constantly using negative words. Maybe they are extremely critical of other people. Maybe they are very pessimistic and are always looking at the negative side of things and telling you why your idea won't work! Stay away from such people because they will only drag you down! Sometimes we need to say no to our old friends and yes to some new friends. Some people don't like the thought of losing their old friends and end up forsaking their dreams instead. But that is their choice. I have never heard of anyone who chose their dreams and regretted it, because the new friends they made on the road to their dreams were of a better calibre and were true friends who supported them.

I once heard a classic response to this at a seminar, when the speaker said, "If you lost your friends because you got involved in this business, you didn't have any to begin with, because a true friend will support you, not discourage you." To which someone else commented, "I maybe lost a few friends, but I've gained a whole lot more." I'm reminded of the story of a woman who tried to please everybody. She wasn't a very happy person and she was constantly stressed out. The reason she wasn't very happy was because she didn't want to say no. People would constantly be asking her favours, to the extent that she hardly had any time left for herself. Although it's good to do people favours and help them out, there has to be a sensible balance between the time we give to others and the time we have for ourselves. Sometimes people would ask her for a loan of money, which she rarely ever saw again. But she continued to loan to them because, more often than not, it was family members and close "friends" who asked her, and she didn't want to offend them or risk being unpopular. But all of this was making her miserable and unhappy because all her efforts were only benefiting other people.

So one day she decided enough was enough and decided to put her foot down. But she didn't make the mistake of going to the other extreme and doing no favours at all. She still did some favours for people, but she also allocated a certain amount of time each day for herself. She decided that no matter how busy she was, nothing and no one was going to eat into this valuable time she had set aside for herself. All chores and favours had to be done outside of this allotted time.

She learned that it was possible to say no in a polite and friendly way, and if people were still offended after that, then it was their problem. For example, someone might say, "Could you give me a hand with the decorating, because I'm hopeless at that." And if she had a full schedule that week, she would say, "Yes I can, but it won't be this week, it will be next week before I get a chance, and it would need to be after 7:00 p.m. because I'm really busy." She didn't actually refuse, but instead she arranged things according to her own schedule and not the schedule other people wanted her to conform to. And if the person said, "Well, it really needs to be done this week because I've got friends coming to stay next week," she simply had to stand her ground in a polite but firm way and say, "That's really unfortunate. I do sympathise with you, but as I said, I'm fully booked up this week. If I had the time I would, but there's simply no way I can fit it in. If I can help you out some other time, please give me a call." And if the person was offended, then it was just too bad. She began to realise that if they were offended, they needed to get a better attitude, not her. Because in life, we are never going to please everyone, so why even try? Nor is everyone always going to like us, but we can ruin our own lives and destroy our own peace of mind by trying to make it so.

for OTHER PEOPLE

Do you realise that people are our biggest asset? Did you ever stop to think about that? It doesn't matter what our ambitions are or what we are trying to do, we need people. If you own a business, you need customers to buy your products or pay for your services. You might even need people to work for you, depending on the size of your business. If you own rental property, you need tenants to provide you with income. If you work for someone, you need an employer; otherwise you will be out of work. The clothes you wear had to be designed and manufactured by someone. The books you read had to be written by someone. If you are into sports, whether it is watching or participating, it involves people. We also need people to speak to when we have problems or need advice. Imagine attending a seminar where no one else was there, not even the speaker. It wouldn't be much fun, would it? It doesn't matter what way we look at it, people are important.

Someone once likened the world to a massive jigsaw puzzle, where each person, great or small, resembled a tiny piece of the puzzle. Each was unique in character and each had their own specific purpose in order to make the picture complete. Without any one piece, no matter how small, the picture would be incomplete. But as much as people are an asset, they can also be our biggest problem. The opposite sex can make us very happy, but occasionally they can give us stress and cause us problems. The only thing that might be harder than dealing with other people is dealing with ourselves. The biggest battle we face is dealing with our emotions. For example, trying to respond positively when someone lets us down, or responding with courage when faced with our fears, or trying to respond positively when someone laughs at our idea and tells us that it won't work. People might be rude to us on the phone when we phone a prospective customer. People might be extremely arrogant or cynical when we share our business idea with them, and we need to be polite and maintain a positive attitude. But as hard as this may be, it is a battle that is well worth winning, because long term, the payoff can be enormous, not just financially, but also in terms of our personal development.

I remember a few years ago setting a business appointment with a guy in town. We both specifically arranged an exact date, time, and place for the appointment so that I could explain the presentation. But when I got there, there was no sign of him. We had only arranged the appointment the day before, so I thought something must have cropped up and he was probably unable to get in touch with me. So I phoned him the next day and he told me that he thought we had arranged it for the following Monday. I was sure that this was not the case, but to give him the benefit of the doubt, just in case there had been a misunderstanding, I said "So are you still interested in looking at the idea? Tell me if you're not because I've got a busy schedule and have a lot of other appointments to set up." He said "Yes! I'm still interested to see what it's about." So we arranged a time to show the presentation the following week.

Again, we confirmed the date, time, and exact location so that there could be no misunderstanding. But when I got there, again there was no sign of him. By now I was beginning to realise that this guy was not interested at all; he just didn't want to say no. So I had to do my best to maintain a positive attitude. Instead of focusing on what had happened,

I had to focus on speaking to the next prospect. We all have a choice when things like that happen.

We can either focus on the problem (the fact that we were let down) or we can focus on the solution (setting up a new appointment with someone else). But it's amazing the amount of people who will focus on the problem and waste vast amounts of time and energy talking about it. They might even allow it to spoil their whole evening, when they could have spent that time and energy finding a new prospect.

Why do I include that example? Because this is part of dealing with people. If you want to become successful, then you're going to have to get used to that kind of stuff. People will test your attitude and your tenacity. The Bible says, "As iron sharpens iron, so one man sharpens another." (Prov 27:17) But as much as we dislike adversity, it is actually beneficial and develops our character.

You might not think it's beneficial at the time, but as you progress, you are changing on the inside, and your self image is improving. Don't forget that what happens to you happens for you. The more of that kind of stuff you are faced with, the better you become at being able to handle it. In other words, your self confidence increases and eventually you get to a point where it hardly even bothers you. You simply accept that it is part of the process of becoming successful.

But it's not all doom and gloom. Remember that people are also our biggest asset and you will also come across people who will have a tremendous positive impact in your life. I am thoroughly convinced that God puts certain people in our lives at certain times for a certain purpose. There will be people who will give you advice and direct you, just when you need it the most. There will be people who will help you become wealthy. There will be people who will give you opportunities. There will be people who build you up and encourage you. There will be people who will give you compliments. There will be people you love and have beautiful relationships with. There will be people who you are forever grateful to and there will be people you will want to forget.

Someone once said, "Everyone brings sunshine to my life; some by coming into it and some by leaving it!" People will test your emotions, and that is probably the hardest part of dealing with people. If you can control your emotions and maintain a positive attitude no matter what other people do, then you are well on your way to becoming successful. If not, then you are in for a rough ride. Some people are like a ship on the ocean. Imagine that they are the ship and other people are the ocean. The ship gets tossed around here, there, and everywhere by the waves, and the waves literally control them. Only in this case they get tossed around emotionally by other people and they allow the actions of other people to control them. Instead of maintaining a positive attitude in the face of adversity, they have mood swings according to how other people treat them. But instead of simply being like a ship on the ocean, we can learn to adjust our rudder and our sails and take control, so that no matter what the waves may do, we can still maintain our course and control our destiny. Your attitude is your rudder and the sails are your emotional response. These things are chosen and are always within your control.

But if people are our biggest asset, then it makes sense that we should learn how to talk to them. A lot of people don't talk to strangers because they're not used to it or they fear being rejected. Sometimes they are afraid of what other people might think of them. But the underlying emotion is usually fear. Remember that the only way to get rid of fear is to do what you're afraid to do. There is no other way. And remember that success is never found inside the comfort zone.

If you don't overcome your fear, then it will control you and you won't move forward. Remember the example of the fleas in the jar? And that they would only jump so high, even with the lid off? Their lid was not real, but psychological.

Well, talking to other people might be your "psychological lid." If it is, then you're not alone, because every one of us have "psychological lids." But the difference between winners and losers is that winners recognise they have a "lid" and they take action in spite of it. Eventually, through repeated acts of courage, the "lid" disappears, and like the fleas in the jar, they can now jump as high as they want. But losers believe that the "lid" cannot come off and refuse to even try. Unfortunately they come to the conclusion that this is one of their limitations in life, and they live out the rest of their lives with the "lid" firmly in place. This is what I call the "great lie." Great because of the magnitude of it and also because of the long term consequences it can have. They have the ability to overcome their fear but they refuse to believe it. They believe a lie instead of the truth, and they allow something imaginary to limit them and steal their dream. How sad. What a waste of potential. It's bad enough allowing something real to limit you, but even worse if it's imagined and fictitious.

A good way to overcome a fear of speaking to people is to go through a step-by-step process. The first step is, the next time you're out somewhere in public or in the street, practice making eye contact and smiling, even if you haven't met them before. Make sure you don't stare or overdo it, but simply look people in the eyes briefly and smile. You could set yourself a goal to smile at a certain amount of people every day. For example, you might decide to smile at twenty people every day. Once you get comfortable doing this, the next step is to say, "Hi" or "Hello." But make sure you're comfortable with one step before moving on to the next. If you're not comfortable, then keep doing it until you do become comfortable. And don't worry if someone doesn't respond; remember, rejection is something that you need to get used to. But it's been my experience that the vast majority of people respond with a smile or a "hello." But even if you do get rejected, what's the worst thing that can happen? Nothing! So what is there to be afraid of?. Once you get used to smiling and saying hello, the next step is to elaborate. For example, you might smile, say hello, and quickly follow up with, "Nice day, isn't it?" or whatever you feel comfortable with. Obviously this step only applies if the person has already smiled or said hello back, otherwise there's no point.

If you smiled and said hello and the person ignored you, they're obviously not interested in talking to you. Or if you make the initial eye contact but they were deliberately avoiding eye contact, then it's pointless trying to start a conversation.

Body language speaks volumes. You can tell a lot about what a person is thinking by their body language. It gives them away every time. Eventually you begin to get a feel for who is friendly and who is not. But getting back to the example of elaborating; if you have made eye contact, smiled, and said hello, and the person has returned all three, then it's up to you what you elaborate on. "Nice day, isn't it?" is just an example, but would only be appropriate if the weather was actually good. At this point, the important thing is to keep it simple. Just a one liner will do. Don't complicate it. Some people choose to comment on something situational, such as something that is going on roundabout them. For example, you might be in a busy shopping mall and say, "It's quite busy today, isn't it?" Some people call this stating the obvious, and it is, but remember, small talk is a very powerful tool and is the bridge between you and actually having a conversation with people. It is also a good way of building rapport with people.

Another example is suppose you're in a shop looking at birthday cards, and someone next to you is also looking at cards. You might say, "I didn't realise they had such a good selection here," or something similar. But the important thing is that you break the ice. But in order to break the ice, you have to be first and you have to risk rejection. It's amazing the amount of people who would just love someone to speak to them. You might be the one who brightens up their day!

So just to re-cap on the original example, you have made eye contact, smiled, said hello, and they have returned all three. You then followed up with, "Nice day, isn't it?" They replied, "Yes, it is." The next step is to ask a question. To master the art of dealing with people, you need to understand the difference between a question and a statement. A statement breaks the ice but doesn't require them to elaborate much. But a question causes them to elaborate and give you information about themselves. This opens up the conversation. "Nice day, isn't it?" is a good icebreaker, but once they reply, "Yes, it is," the conversation dies, unless you keep it going by asking questions. Some people can talk for ages if you ask them the right questions. So what are the right questions? Well, firstly we need to recognise that people are primarily interested in themselves, not you. So if you ask people questions about themselves and their interests, you are talking about their favorite subject. All you have to do is listen and ask the occasional question. If you said, "Nice day, isn't it?" and they said, "Yes it is," you could then follow up with a question, such as "Have you got a busy schedule today?" (Notice how the question includes the word "you.") This will then lay the foundation for opening up a conversation, and they might proceed to tell you about their schedule for that day. Or, if we take the example of being in a card shop looking at cards and you said, "I didn't realise they had such a good selection here," (statement) and they respond with something like, "Yes, they have a really good selection," you could then ask a question such as, "Have you got some birthdays coming up?" And often they will start to tell you about all the presents they've still to buy and all the things they've still to do. That's the power of asking questions. But none of this would have happened if you hadn't broken the ice. So, an ice breaker first (statement), and if you get a favourable response, then a question. If you said, "I didn't realise they had such a good selection here," and they just kind of grunted, then there's obviously no point in going any further.

You can judge whether people are interested in having a conversation or not by their response. If a person simply gives rigid yes or no answers then it becomes more like an interrogation than anything else. But if a person is eager to talk about themselves, and most people are, then you will only have to listen, and they will do most of the talking. But if a person answers your question and also asks you questions in return, this is the ideal situation and they are clearly interested in talking to you. Questions equal interest, lack of questions equal lack of interest. But all of this started with just a smile and making eye contact, remember? So just to clarify everything, here is a summary of the ideal situation. Obviously things won't always work out like this and won't always go as planned, but this is kind of like a blueprint that you can use as an example:

YOU: make eye contact and smile
THEY: make eye contact and smile

YOU: say, "Hello."
THEY: say, "Hello."

YOU: say, "Nice day isn't it?"
THEY: say, "Yes it is."

YOU: Say, "Have you got a busy schedule today?" or a similar question.
THEY: Go into a detailed explanation of all the things they have to do that day. You only need to listen and ask the occasional question.

But if this is new territory for you, don't let it overwhelm you and don't try and do it all at once. Practice getting used to one step at a time. You may want to spend weeks, or even months practicing a single step. That way you can build up confidence at each level. The more you practice this, the easier it gets. So how will all of this information benefit us? It will benefit us not only in making business contacts but also in our social lives and our own personal development. Not only that, but it also reduces your fear of people because by doing what you fear, you begin to destroy fear.

for PERSISTENCE

What do you do when everything seems to go against you? What do you do when life seems unfair and success seems like a million miles away? What do you do when you're putting in huge amounts of effort and can see no reward? What do you do when other people are succeeding but you're getting rejection after rejection? What do you do when you're faced with fear, and the doubts start to creep in? What do you do when people are ridiculing you and telling you that your stupid idea won't work? Do you persist or do you quit? Do you listen to them or do you ignore them? The answer to that will determine your future.

Persistence, or lack of it, is what separates winners from losers. It doesn't matter how educated or intelligent you are; if you don't have the guts to persist, then none of that matters. When faced with adversity, we come to a fork in the road. We either persist or quit. There is no alternative road or third choice. Yes it is true that some people put things on hold because they're going through a tough time, but eventually the choice will be made. From what I've observed, the vast majority of people who put things on hold usually end up quitting. Putting things on hold is usually a temporary way of trying to avoid the pain of choosing. But that's not how the battle is won. It is only won by persevering against all odds that you become successful. You will never break down an obstacle or gain self confidence by avoiding it. The only way to triumph over an obstacle is to face it again and again. There is no other way. Sure, you may need to change your approach or change tactics, but don't give up.

When you run from an obstacle or even put it on hold, it tends to get bigger and causes fear. At least, that's what happens in our minds. This causes our inner self talk to become negative, and we usually end up talking ourselves out of our own dreams and quitting. But if you face the obstacle head-on, as painful as it may be, your inner self talk is still positive, because you know you're doing the right thing and you are still in pursuit of your dreams. You know that the obstacle cannot and will not last forever.

As long as you persist, the obstacle is eventually doomed to crumble. The obstacle may last longer than anticipated and it may be tougher than expected, but as long as you persist, you will eventually succeed. To put it another way, you are either in the business of running from obstacles or overcoming obstacles. When you are in the business of overcoming obstacles, you are in the business of persistence. Each time you overcome an obstacle, your self confidence increases, but if you run from it or try to avoid it, you lose self confidence. You cannot gain self confidence unless you experience something.

But as tough as your situation may be, even adversity can be looked at in a positive light, because the greater the pain, the greater your reward will be. The greater the adversity, the greater the benefits that come from it. Great success is always preceded by great adversity. The higher the mountain, the deeper the valley. But it's worth it. The Bible says, "And we rejoice in the hope of the glory of God. Not only so, but we also rejoice in our sufferings, because we know that suffering produces perseverance; perseverance, character; and character, hope." (Rom 5:2-4).

Hope! That's what persistence gives us! Because we know that as long as we persist, we are still on the road to success. As long as we are battling against our obstacles, we still have hope!

Unfortunately there are a lot of hopeless people out there, either because they've quit or because they didn't have any goals to begin with. We are either going forwards or going backwards. If we have goals and are actively pursuing them, we are going forwards, but if we don't have any goals, or have goals but are not pursuing them, we are going backwards.

Some people claim that life is unfair, and I must admit, I agree. But life isn't only unfair to you, life is unfair to everybody. So don't think you're being singled out. If you're going through something tough, you're going through it for a reason. God may be trying to teach you something or refine your behaviour in some way, or eliminate some bad habits, but long term it's going to be beneficial. Remember, life was never meant to be fair, so don't expect it to be. It's not what happens to you, but how you handle it that counts. Sometimes you see absolutely no reward for your efforts, at least not just now. But that will be compensated for later on.

Eventually things will become clear to you, even if they make no sense just now. After a certain period of time you will begin to see how important those trials were. You will look at them differently (usually in hindsight), and instead of remembering the pain they caused, you will appreciate the valuable lessons they taught you. When you look at them in that way, you will realise that success would not have been possible without them. You may even get to a point where you eventually thank God for them. But I have to be completely honest here; I thank God for the trials in my past now, but I wasn't thanking Him at the time. At the time I actually thought He didn't care. It took me a good few years to fully realise that these trials were not sent to punish me or to make me miserable, which was what I thought at the time, but they were sent to forever alter the course of my life in a way that I could never have imagined possible. The problem is, we don't think like God and He doesn't think like us.

> "'For my thoughts are not your thoughts,
> neither are your ways my ways,' declares the
> Lord. 'As the heavens are higher than the earth,
> so are my ways higher than your ways and my
> thoughts than your thoughts.'" (Isaiah 55:8-9)

Sometimes you may feel abandoned by God, but realise that God will never abandon you. If God has put you in that situation, He's put you in it for a reason. God wants you to change. He knows we cannot be successful in our present form, and God wants us to be extremely successful. If you are in a tough situation, it could be because when you get through it, you can help other people get through it. God may want to use you. This is also part of His plan for your life. "For I know the plans I have for you," declares the Lord, "plans to prosper you and not to harm you, plans to give you hope and a future." (Jer 29:11).

The other thing to remember is that success is not always logical. Sometimes you need to do what seems illogical at the time. You may have to take a step backwards in order to go a few steps forward. But no one likes going backwards, and you may feel as though temporarily you are losing the battle. Sometimes you need to lose temporarily in order to win long term. You may need to lose a few battles in order to win the war. But it's worth it. Don't give up after losing a battle; learn from it and move on. When the Allied forces landed on the beaches of Normandy, there were horrendous casualties, but there was no going back. Even when the beaches were declared secure and they moved inland, there were some ferocious battles ahead. There were successes and defeats, but they pressed on regardless. And ultimately, they won.

Sometimes in life we are faced with tough decisions and we are not sure which way to go. We may be faced with a variety of options and have to go through a process of trial and error and risk further defeat. This calls for courage. Whenever you put yourself in a position where you risk defeat or humiliation, it calls for courage. Some people prefer to call this a process of elimination, but the principle is still the same. We examine all of our options and then decide on a course of action, but we're not sure whether this is the best option or not. This can be painful because sometimes these courses of action can be absolute failures and humiliating defeats. But they are essential because we need to know what is on the other side; success or failure. And only by eliminating our options will we find out. In other words, we have to go through it. We need to be willing to risk defeat and risk looking bad in order to win. Not many people are willing to risk defeat, therefore not many people achieve great success. Average people avoid pain, but successful people endure it and also learn from it.

When it comes to persistence, there are only two participants, you and the obstacle. One of you is going to win and one of you is going to lose. It's a bit like a duel in the sky between two fighter pilots. They cannot both survive. One will live and one will die. But the advantage you have is that you can choose to survive; the obstacle cannot. Your secret weapons are persistence and endurance. You have advantages over the obstacle. As big as the obstacle is, it cannot get any bigger, but you can. Therefore, as you persist, the obstacle gradually loses its power and begins to get smaller. Eventually it dies and simply becomes another one of your great teachers on the road to success.

Sometimes our obstacles can be long, drawn-out affairs that call for endurance. Others may be over relatively quickly but are far more painful. But it's how we respond to them that matters. Our response is everything. There's no point in wishing they hadn't happened, because that won't change anything. Instead, concentrate on the solution and figure out a positive response.

Sometimes we are struggling because we are going through a process of change. Change usually involves getting rid of our old negative habits and replacing them with positive ones. This is usually an emotional battle and will probably be one of the hardest things you will ever do, especially if you have had these habits most of your life. When you give up habits that you've had for a lifetime and take on new positive habits, you're going into unknown territory, and that can be scary. You don't know what's ahead of you or what will be expected of you. You just have to go on sheer faith and take advice from people who have already gone before you. This is when you need a mentor. You need someone who's already blazed a trail through the area you're going into.

Emotional battles can often cause people to quit because they're so painful. No one likes pain, but everyone wants the rewards. Persistence is the only answer. All obstacles get smaller if you persist and face them head on. What seems like a mountain just now will eventually seem like a molehill if you persist. The Bible tells us, "If you have faith as small as a mustard seed, you can say to this mountain, 'Move from here to there,' and it will move. Nothing will be impossible for you." (Mat 17:20) Someone once said that tragedy plus time equals humour. And when I first heard that I thought, "What on earth is he talking about?" because at the time I heard it, I was in the middle of what was a tragedy to me, and I couldn't see any way out. Neither did I see any humour in it, because I was depressed.

I thought to myself, "Even if I do get through this and live to be a hundred years old, I will never find this humorous!" The thought of quitting had entered my mind, not just because of the pain of the situation, but because I thought I was in a hopeless situation with no way out. But understand that God will never put you in a hopeless situation. It may seem hopeless at the time, but there's a purpose to it; usually a purpose we cannot see. But He sees everything and knows everything. I was in a seminar and I was kind of ticked off when I heard the speaker say that, because I thought to myself, "It's alright for him! He's saying that through ignorance. If he knew my situation he wouldn't be saying that! How can he talk about humour when I'm going through hell?" But looking back now, I can see the sense in what he said, and he was right. I also made the mistake of assuming that he had achieved success easily and thinking that I was the only one with problems.

How naive! I was probably thinking about how successful he was at the time and didn't realise that he had been through his own struggles. That's obviously why he was successful and why he was on the stage! He was further down the road than I was and had probably been through what I was going through.

When you are going through struggles, what you feed your mind is paramount. Some people call them the "big three:" what you listen to, what you read, and who you associate with. These three things, in the vast majority of cases, often mean the difference between success and failure. People who succeed learn to control their thoughts by only allowing positivity into their minds. People who fail (or quit) have usually allowed their thoughts to become negative by failing to control what goes into their minds. As a result, they talk themselves out of their own dreams. Let me give you an example: suppose someone is expanding a business and they are having a tough time in every sense of the word. Nothing is going right, yet they are putting in massive effort. Life doesn't seem fair, and the doubts are starting to creep in. So they decide to talk to someone. But they have a choice. They can either speak to someone in the business who is more experienced than they are and who has a vested interest in their success, or they can speak to their best friend.

The only problem is that, although their "friend" means well, their "friend" is extremely negative and cynical about their business. Their "friend" has never been in business in their life, neither does their "friend" have any goals or ambitions. Who do you think is the best person to listen to? Who do you think will give them the best advice? I think the answer is obvious. Sadly, many people choose to listen to their "friends'" advice. They don't think logically and take advice based on how successful the person is. Instead they make an emotional decision and listen to who they feel closest to.

Their "friend" might say something like, "I told you that business was no good! You'll lose all your money. Don't get involved!" As a result, they quit. Yet if they had spoken to someone in the business who had already achieved what they were trying to achieve and had already been through what they were going through, they could have pointed them in the right direction and guided them through it. Instead, they allowed their "friend" to steal their dream. Their decision to persist or quit was based on who they took their advice from. In short, they actually allowed that person to control their future.

But what we listen to is also very important. Someone might be in the exact same situation, having a hard time and having doubts and be feeling emotionally down. At a time like this, what they need is something to lift them up emotionally, not drag them down further. And the only way to do that is by listening to something which will cause them to have positive emotions. So they have a choice. They could listen to the radio and hear all kinds of bad news and horror stories about people getting ripped off, or they could listen to a motivational CD and hear how someone who was faced with a similar situation overcame their struggles despite the odds being stacked against them. Two different choices, resulting in two different thought processes. One choice depresses them even further, causing doubt and fear. The other choice gives them hope. Every time you allow something into your mind, you always want to be asking yourself, "What kind of emotional impact will this have? Will it cause positive or negative emotions?" And then act accordingly.

What you read also plays a huge part in helping you to persist. But you also need to be aware of the difference between positive and negative literature. If you read a newspaper, it's virtually impossible to finish the paper and still be thinking about your dreams. It's also virtually impossible to finish the paper and be filled with positive emotions, such as joy, hope, faith, or enthusiasm. So why do it? Instead of taking you closer to your dreams, it will take you further away and will make you more pessimistic. It will probably destroy all of your positive emotions and replace them with negative emotions such as doubt, fear, worry, and possibly anger (depending on what you read). Your mind will be filled with so many negative thoughts and emotions that your dreams will seem like they are a million miles away. Therefore it makes sense to read from a positive thinking book if you want to be happy and successful. But amazingly, most people don't do that. This simple but important choice can often mean the difference between persistence and giving up, or achieving your dreams and not achieving them. Make the wise choice; read something positive.

"It is impossible to achieve victory unless you dare to do battle." (Craig Deane)

"I consider that our present sufferings are not worth comparing with the glory that will be revealed in us." (Rom 8:18)

for QUESTIONS

Did you know that whoever asks the question controls the conversation? It's not the person who does the most talking, but who does the most listening who is in control. And the way to do that is to ask questions and listen. Not ask questions and talk, but ask questions and be quiet. Let them talk. I mean really pay attention to what they are saying, not just wait for a gap to speak again. Words such as why, who, when, how, where, what, and which are all very powerful words because they put you in control. The reason they put you in control is that they require the other person to give you information. That's why during a job interview it can be quite intimidating, because the people doing the interviewing are asking the questions and they are in total control. Usually there is more than one person doing the interviewing. Often one person is asking the questions and the person next to them is listening intently, possibly taking notes and also watching your body language. In other words, you are being put on the spot.

But during an ordinary conversation the person doing the least amount of talking is usually in control. The person asking the questions and listening is getting a lot of information from the other person. They are also choosing the subject about which they will talk by the very nature of the questions they ask. Therefore they can direct the conversation in any way they want. If they want the conversation to be about business, they will ask a question about how that person's business is going, and this will set the tone for the conversation. If they want the conversation to be about cars, they might compliment that person's car and ask them questions relating to their car. For example, they might comment on how smart it looks and ask them how long they've had it. Some people will talk for ages if you just ask them the right questions. You don't have to do much except stand there and listen and ask the occasional question. But what are the right questions? I'll answer that for you in one sentence: THEMSELVES and THEIR INTERESTS!

NOT you and your interests, which is what most people do. People are extremely interested in themselves. If you want to get on well with other people, you need to under-stand human nature and learn to become extremely inter-ested in their interests and what's important to them. It has been said that a person is more interested in a spot on their face than a disaster in a foreign country that kills hundreds of people. Think about it, if someone suddenly showed you an old school photo which included you, who is the first person you would look for in the photo? Do you get my point?

By asking people questions about themselves, you are talking about their favourite subject. Asking them questions about their interests is equally effective. For example, if you know someone likes cars, it's a good idea to take an interest in THEIR car instead of talking about yours. If you know they like golf, you might want to ask them what courses they play on, or how often they play. Asking questions about someone else's children, and how they're getting on, is an-other good subject, because you are talking about something extremely important to them. This not only shows you are interested in them as a person, but it also helps to keep the conversation going. This will win you friends, and you will be perceived as an interesting person. Remember what we said earlier, that to have a friend, you first must be a friend?

Well, asking someone questions about themselves is an excellent way to start.

But what we say depends on the situation. Each situation is different, and what is appropriate in one situation might not be appropriate in another. We might be sitting next to someone in a restaurant and strike up a conversation with them. Suppose we are expanding a business and are looking to recruit new people, we might want to find out more about this person and their level of ambition. Even if they didn't qualify or weren't interested, they might be able to lead us to people who do qualify. But rather than just starting asking questions about business right away, it's a lot better if we take an interest in them as a person and find out more about them. It also puts other people at ease if you introduce yourself and ask their name; otherwise people might think, "This person isn't really interested in me; they're only interested in business." Obviously, if it is a total stranger, you might want to start with small talk first, before asking their name, otherwise they might find it a bit odd, you suddenly asking their name as an opening line. For example, you might open the conversation by commenting on what they're eating and say, "That looks good. I see you eat very healthily." And by their response you can tell a lot about how friendly they are, or how willing they are to have a conversation. If they just sort of grunt and don't say much, there's no point going any further. But if they seem talkative and friendly enough, you might follow up with a question such as, "Are you from around here, or are you on holiday?" And if the conversation progresses, you could then say, "By the way, my name is— (and introduce yourself). And if you didn't quite catch their name, you could say, "Sorry, what was your name?"

If they are quite talkative and this leads to a good conversation, you might only need to ask the occasional question and they will do most of the talking. Once you have established good rapport with them, then it might be more appropriate to ask some business questions. By asking questions, you can then find out if this person would qualify for your business (or if they know someone who would qualify). But as important as questions are, we also need to recognise the importance of silence. As soon as we ask a question, we need to be quiet and listen. Don't ask a question and then answer for them, which is what some people do. Ask a question and pay attention to what they are actually saying. Don't interrupt, and wait until they are finished before you start speaking. A good motto is "quick to listen, slow to speak."

Usually, if they are willing to talk, asking questions will provide the fuel for a good conversation. If they are genuinely interested in talking to you, they will ask questions in return. This is the ideal situation, because remember that questions equal interest; lack of questions equals lack of interest. Think about it, if you see someone you are attracted to, don't you want to ask them questions and find out more about them? But just to summarise on the original example, you are sitting next to someone in a restaurant and the conversation goes something like this:

> YOU: "That looks good. I see you eat very healthily." (statement/ice breaker)

> THEM: "Oh yes, it's my favourite. I like to treat myself now and again"

> YOU: "Are you from around here or are you on holiday?" (question)

> THEM: "I actually stay in town, but we come here once in a while because we quite like it here."

> YOU: "Yeah, we like it here too. The food is really good and so is the service. By the way, my name is— . What's your name?"

THEM: "My name is— . Good to meet you. What about you, are you from around here?"

— and so the conversation continues. Notice that as soon as they told you their name and said, "Good to meet you," they quickly followed up with a question, asking if you were also from that area. The fact that they have asked you a question in return is a good sign, and shows that they are genuinely interested in talking to you. But if a person just kept answering your questions without asking you any in return, there's a high chance that they could simply be being polite and are not really interested in talking to you. But if they do seem interested in talking to you, you might want to ask other questions, such as, "Have you always lived here?" or "What do you do for a living?"

Now that you have gotten to know a little bit about them, this is when you can start to shift the conversation on to business, if you so desire. Once they have told you what they do for a living, the next step is to find out if they are satisfied or not. If they are not satisfied, you can then ask them if they are looking for opportunities. So how do you find out if someone is satisfied with their work or not? One way is to ask them if they like what they do; another way is to compliment it and build it up. If they're not satisfied, they'll soon tell you. Let them tear it down. Don't you do that! Then listen to what they say. For example, if they say, "I'm a long distance lorry driver," you could compliment it by saying, "You must enjoy getting to visit all the different towns." And if they like what they do, they will agree with you. But if they don't like it they might say something like, "Yeah, but the pay is terrible," or "Yeah, but I sure get fed up sitting behind the wheel all day." If they express dissatisfaction, or say something negative about their work, the next step is to ask a question and bring it out of them. You could say, "Do you ever consider looking at business opportunities or ways to make extra money," to which they will answer yes or no. If they say, "Yes, I'm always looking," you can then proceed to tell them about the business you're expanding, or if they say no, you haven't lost anything either.

If you want good answers, you need to ask intelligent questions. Poor questions yield poor answers. For example, if one was dissatisfied with their work and you thought they might qualify to be a recruit in your business, intelligent questions might include the following:

"Have you ever considered owning your own business?"

"If you have considered it but haven't done it, what stopped you?"

"If I could show you a way of raising capital, would you want to know it?"

"What are your prospects if you keep doing what you're doing?"

"Where do you see yourself five years from now?"

The person is then being forced to think about it. They might never have thought about it before, until you asked the question. I'll never forget the time I was at an open opportunity meeting and the speaker said, "Is there anybody here tonight who has thought about owning their own business in the past, but for some reason, something has prevented them from doing it?" And a whole sea of hands went up. He then picked some of them at random and asked them what kind of business they had considered and what their reasons were for not starting. There was a whole range of answers and a whole load of reasons for not starting, such as, "I didn't think there would be a good enough market for it." or "I thought it would be too risky." But the main reason was lack of capital. He then picked this one guy and said, "You sir! What kind of business did you think of starting?" And he said, "A waterskiing club." And the speaker said, "And what prevented you from starting?" And he said "The water was too cold," and the room just erupted with laughter.

But striking up conversations is not just limited to restaurants. Waiting rooms, shopping malls, trains, airplanes, and all forms of public transport are just a few examples of where we meet people. In fact, anywhere outside your home you are likely to meet people. When you fill the car up with petrol you meet people. Even when you're at home, you occasionally meet new people. For example, someone comes to read the electric meter or deliver your mail. These are all opportunities to find out more about them by asking questions. We must also remember that compliments are excellent ice breakers. For example, if you see someone wearing something that's extremely eye catching, let them know. Tell them you like it, and then follow up with a question, such as "I hope you don't mind me asking, but where did you get it?" This is also an excellent way to start a conversation. People love to get compliments; don't you?

I once heard someone talk about what they called the "bus stop syndrome," where everyone stands together but no one talks to each other. It also happens in waiting rooms and elevators. These are all potential opportunities to start conversations and ask questions. He said, "Isn't it amazing, when you're in an elevator and it's packed with people, that most people stand and silently watch the floor indicators changing, without saying a word? Occasionally there's someone who stands with their back to the door and faces everyone." The point he was making is that these are all opportunities to start conversations by asking questions. You might start with a statement such as, "It's a busy place today," and then follow up with a question such as, "Have you worked here for long," or "Which floor do you work on?" These are all situations where small talk comes in handy. Simple questions like these can often lead to good friendships or even relationships! Who knows? But the important thing is that you break the ice. Don't worry if it doesn't lead anywhere or if the person doesn't seem talkative. Remember, you are creating a habit (one that will serve you well), and you can't turn habits on and off. When you get used to doing something, you tend to do it all the time, because it's done subconsciously. The subconscious doesn't distinguish from person to person. The way you program your subconscious is how it will operate when dealing with "all" persons. Make a habit of talking to everyone, not just the ones you think are "important." If you don't bother to talk to someone because you don't think they are important to you, you have missed a chance to improve your skills; skills you will wish you had when the important time arises. Look upon talking to everyone as your training ground; each person an opportunity. When you've done something often enough (such as breaking the ice), you will eventually start to act that way without even thinking about it. If the person doesn't say anything back, at least you've gotten out of your comfort zone, and this will help to reduce your fear of people. Breaking the ice is also good for your self image and building your self confidence, so that even if you are rejected you gain something. This also makes it easier to do the next time. But eventually, once you've done it often enough, you actually begin to enjoy striking up conversations. What you once had fear of, you now enjoy. The mind will get used to anything. It's at this point that you have created a new comfort zone. Well done!

BEING ASKED QUESTIONS

Sometimes we might find ourselves in situations where we're being bombarded with questions. For example, if we're explaining a business presentation to a group of people, we might get all kinds of questions thrown at us. Unless we're mentally prepared for it, it can seem intimidating. Often the questions being asked are legitimate questions which indicate interest, but sometimes we might come across someone who is not very polite and asks questions that you feel are too personal. In that case you could answer a question with a question. You could say (depending on the question), "Why do you ask that?" or you could be more subtle about it. For example, if they say "How much money are you making?" you could say, "What I make will have no bearing on how much you could make, therefore I don't want to limit you by telling you how much I make, in case I slow you down. What matters is what you do with the opportunity and how much effort you put in." That answer, although vague, is perfectly truthful, and you are not lying. Some people call this "answering it but not answering it."

In addition to that response, you could also back it up with a question such as, "Can you just remind me of what it was you wanted to achieve when you first saw this opportunity?" By doing this you have just regained control of the conversation. Remember, he who asks the question controls the conversation. They had the control to begin with by asking you a question, but you answered their question and then turned it around and took the control back. But it may not stop at that. Some people keep going and ask more questions. In that case, you simply repeat the process and employ the same tactics until they get fed up with asking questions. Some people call this "The broken record technique." Although the questions you ask them in return might vary, the strategy is the same. And if they keep asking the same questions, you could begin your answer with, "As I said before—."

And if they keep pressing you, "Like I've always said—."

The key is to answer their question as briefly as possible and then ask them a question, which takes the focus off of you and puts it back onto them. If you ask them a question about something that's important to them such as, "What do you want to achieve," it will take their mind off of what they were asking you in the first place. And while you are in control, you could ask further questions, such as, "What do you do for a living," or "Have you done it for long," or "Do you have a family?" All of these things keep you in control.

I think we are all well aware that politicians (as much as we might disagree with them) have mastered the art of not answering the question. I'm not saying it's right that they do this, because most of the questions they're asked are legitimate questions, asked by people they are supposed to represent and are being paid well for it. In fact, some politicians are devious and downright deceitful. But in a business environment where we are not deceiving anyone, we may need to employ certain tactics if we are being bombarded with questions or being asked questions that we think we shouldn't be getting asked.

for REST AND RELAXATION

Believe it or not, but the time we spend relaxing is just as important as the time we spend at work. If we want to live long, happy lives and stay in good health, there needs to be a sensible balance between work and play. I say sensible because if we take too much time off, we will never reach our goals, but if we don't take enough time off, we are in danger of burning ourselves out and destroying our health. Both extremes are bad and lead to failure. Therefore you need to decide what feels right for you. It's similar to working out at the gym. If you were to keep exercising without stopping, you would eventually collapse from exhaustion. On the other hand, if you were to sit around talking most of the time and didn't do much exercise, you would never get fit. Once again, it's the sensible balance that determines your success.

Some people feel guilty if they have some time off, but it is usually the people who feel guilty that need it the most. They are usually the ones who are classed as "workaholics" and often deprive themselves of any kind of reward for their efforts. But it's during the time off that we're being recharged for doing the work. Imagine for a moment a rechargeable battery; how long do you think it would last if you were to charge it fully, one time, and never ever charge it again? It wouldn't last very long, even if it was the best quality battery on the market. Every now and again it has to be recharged in order to be useful. Only by doing this will it come anywhere near its potential, in terms of productivity. It's the same with us.

But having time off doesn't necessarily mean going on a two-week vacation or a three-month cruise, although there is nothing wrong with that if that's what you want. In fact, for many people, that is simply part of the reward for their efforts. But in terms of day-to-day living, we can sometimes feel fatigued or worn out simply due to the stresses and strains of life. This is when even a brief period of rest can make all the difference. If you take five minutes out of your busy schedule to simply sit still, close your eyes, relax all your muscles and try to think of nothing, you will be amazed at how much better you feel. This will also help to re-energise you. Simply sitting still with your eyes shut will help you to relax your muscles and will save twenty-five percent of your energy, because a quarter of all our energy is used up through the eyes. That's why reading and driving long distances can cause us to feel tired. Ironically, the busier we are, the more important it is to reward ourselves with periods of rest and relaxation. Some people claim that they haven't got time to rest because there's too much to do, but they fail to realise that that is exactly why they need to do it. The busier someone is, the higher the chance of burnout if they don't take a break. Apart from anything else, life isn't much fun if it's all about work!

People have different ways of relaxing. For some people, just sitting doing nothing is a good way to relax. Some people might like to listen to soft tranquil music, while others prefer silence. Others might like to read a book. Some people might like to be alone, while others prefer to spend time with their friends or watch a TV program. It's all a matter of personal choice. Some people have a day job and go out to work again in the evening. Granted, they may not have a lot of time in between, but at some point in the day, even if it is late in the evening, they need to have some quality time for themselves. This quality time isn't found, it's made. There's a difference! You need to make it a priority.

Some people neglect their relationships because of work, but what good is money if it's at the expense of your relationships? What's more important? Only you can answer that. Of course we are all very busy and there's nothing wrong with hard work, but the danger is when it becomes all work and no play. Remember, balance is the key. Perhaps your idea of switching off is going for a swim or a Jacuzzi with your spouse. Or it could just be hanging out down at the fitness club, where you can temporarily forget about everything. Switching off mentally is just as important as switching off physically. Maybe your idea of relaxing is playing golf? If so, why not reward yourself with a game of golf every now and again? Why not cut out pictures of your favourite golf courses and put them somewhere you will see them every day and use it as a form of motivation?

If your idea of relaxing is playing golf, why not set yourself a goal to do a certain amount of work and then reward yourself with a game of golf? Once you've had your game of golf, set another goal to do a certain amount of work and reward yourself with something else. You may want to reward yourself monthly so that every month you and your spouse do something special together and stick to it. It could be something as simple as dining out, so that no one has to do the cooking or washing up. It could be to go on a trip somewhere and stay in one of your favourite hotels. Maybe you like boats and you find it peaceful being out on the water. Perhaps you like the countryside and like to get away from all the noise of being in town. Imagine being out in the country, where there's no traffic and the only noises to be heard are running water from a nearby river and the wildlife. You can smell the freshness of the trees and you feel totally at peace. Work is the furthest thing from your mind. You are totally relaxed.

But the important thing is that you constantly have

something in front of you, as a reward for your efforts. It's so easy to say you're going to do it and then forget, or put it off, so I recommend writing down whatever you and your spouse agree to do, and how often you are going to do it, and then put it somewhere that you will both see it every day. Not only will it stop you from forgetting, but it will also act as motivation and remind you that life is not only about work. When you have something to look forward to, it even makes your work seem more exciting, and you will be more enthusiastic.

GETTING ENOUGH SLEEP

Another important part of rest is making sure that we get enough sleep. For it is during sleep that our bodies recharge themselves and the healing process can take place more rapidly because there is no interference from our conscious minds. When we are awake, negative thinking can adversely affect the workings of our subconscious mind. Our negative thoughts create negative emotions which disrupt the work-ings of the subconscious and prevents it from working harmoniously. Vital processes are disrupted and this can result in having an adverse effect on our physical bodies. During sleep, the processes which take place are subcon-scious, free from conscious thought, and operate automati-cally. For example, we still continue to breathe, our heart continues to beat, our hair continues to grow, and the body continues to heal itself without any conscious thought. Therefore it is vital that we do not deprive our bodies of the sleep they need so that these vital processes can take place. Although the human brain needs a certain amount of sleep, our muscles do not require sleep; they only require physical rest in order to reenergise themselves.

Different people require varying amounts of sleep, usually ranging from between four to eight hours. It has been proven that people who think they need eight hours can usually get by and operate just as effectively on six hours. I am proof of that, since I used to be convinced that I needed eight hours. A lot of these beliefs stem from what we tell ourselves. Not only that, but they also stem from what teachers and parents tell us. If you tell yourself that you must get eight hours' sleep or you will be "shattered" the next day, then that will be true for you because that is what you believe. Remember, your subconscious creates according to belief, not according to facts. Therefore it will create in your body what you tell it.

If you believe that you only need six hours' sleep, then that will also be true for you, because that is what you believe. I used to believe that if I got less than eight hours' sleep, or if I wasn't asleep by a certain time, I would be shattered the next day. As a result I was shattered, because that's how I had programmed my mind and that's what I told myself. Some people actually talk about it in conversation and say things like, "I'm shattered. I only got four hours' sleep last night." And all they're doing is reinforcing it and making themselves feel worse. Why program yourself to feel worse by telling yourself you feel shattered if you don't have to? But it is equally important to realise that I 'm not suggesting depriving the body or pushing it to the limit, or anything which could potentially cause harm. What I am saying is that most people don't need as much sleep as they think they need.

Most people could get by on less and still function just as effectively. This is what I call the "optimum amount," which I mentioned in my first book, You Are the Problem, You Are the Solution. The optimum amount simply means the minimum amount of sleep required while still being able to function and operate with maximum effectiveness.

In other words, this amount is not too much or too little. It is simply the right amount for you. The optimum amount is different for everyone, and you need to find out what is right for you. I didn't suddenly cut down my sleep from eight hours to six overnight. I cut it down gradually, over a period of months, a little bit at a time. Eventually I came to a point where I would begin to feel fatigued if I went below it. I realised this was my "optimum amount." I also realised that my original belief of "I must have eight hours or I will be shattered" must have been false, otherwise I would not have been able to cut it down. But remember, you are only human; you are not a machine, and common sense should always prevail when finding your optimum amount.

But our energy levels are not just affected by the amount of sleep we get; our habits also have an effect on our energy levels. Habits that cause positive emotions strengthen us and increase our energy, but habits that cause negative emotions drain our energy and can cause us to require more sleep. For example, immoral sexual habits resulting in the negative emotion of lust, drain our energy and sap our physical strength. Any kind of sexual immorality or doing what you believe is wrong will have an adverse affect on your body. "He who sins sexually, sins against his own body." (1 Cor 6:18).

Worrying also wastes a lot of energy and can affect us physically. This can require us to need more sleep. We might feel "drained" as a result of worrying. That's why we've all heard the saying "worried sick," because of the powerful effect the mind has on the body. If we are stressed out, this can also cause us to have poor quality sleep, because negative emotions are operating subconsciously, even during sleep. Anything that operates at a subconscious level, such as our emotions, is a continuous process and never stops. We cannot switch our emotions off; we can only give them direction by changing them from negative to positive, and the way to do that is by changing our habits and changing what goes into our minds. Negative emotions caused by stress or worry may cause insomnia or even nightmares. Only when our emotions are positive will we be relaxed and improve the quality of our sleep. But we cannot simply "get rid" of a negative emotion; it has to be replaced, because we are always thinking something.

If you're worrying, it's very hard to "try" to stop worrying, because what you're doing is trying to pit your tiny conscious thinking against the mighty subconscious, and the subconscious always wins. Instead, it would be better to replace what was in your subconscious by reading from a positive book. This is especially important if you find yourself worrying at night, just before going to bed. The last thoughts you have before going to sleep will be more readily absorbed by your subconscious, because your subconscious is free from all conscious thought during sleep. That's why, if you were to watch something depressing on TV, such as the news or a violent film just before going to bed, you might still feel depressed in the morning. The same applies if you were to have an argument just before going to sleep. In fact, anything which causes you to have negative emotions will have the same effect.

Some people worry if they can't get to sleep and they worry if they've not had enough sleep. But this is futile, because worrying about not getting to sleep is more likely to keep you awake. It's better to simply accept the fact that your body doesn't want to sleep at the moment (accepting it instead of fighting it), and this will give you peace of mind and you will be more relaxed. And if you still don't fall asleep, deliberately force yourself to think pleasant thoughts. Resist the temptation to worry or think negative thoughts. Recall the happiest and most beautiful moments in your life, and dwell on these thoughts instead. Forget about the time and refuse to look at the clock again. Turn it the other way. I've never heard of anyone who died from a lack of sleep. If your body wants it badly enough, you'll soon fall asleep. That's why people fall asleep at the wheel when driving. But there are other alternatives if you can't sleep. For example, I've known myself to get up and read for an hour. I figured that I might as well do something constructive rather than just lie there doing nothing. Another idea is to listen to some soft music. If you have an iPod, you might want to use the earphones and listen to some of your favourite music. Some people have been known to get up and do a little exercising, in order to "tire themselves" into sleeping. But these are just suggestions, and it's up to you what you do.

If you find yourself worrying because you didn't get enough sleep, realise that this is also futile and counter-productive. Worrying will do more damage to you than the actual loss of sleep itself. Instead of worrying, forget about it, because you are creating negative emotions. You can always catch up on your sleep the next again night. People who go around telling other people that they feel "shattered" because they only got a few hours' sleep are programming their subconscious mind to fail by giving it negative in-structions. Instead, they could choose to program their subconscious with positive emotions by telling themselves and other people that they feel great, even if they don't. By doing that, they can only feel better because the subcon-scious doesn't care about "facts;" it simply does what it's told. No matter how little sleep you've had or what you're up against physically, always program your subconscious for success. This is something that's within your control and always will be. Someone once said, "If you're going to lack sleep, you may as well lack it positively."

The best antidote for stress is relaxation. Relaxation is the opposite of stress. You cannot feel both at the same time. Tests have shown that we cannot experience fear or any other negative emotion while our muscles are totally re-laxed. Have you ever wondered why some people seem to be more laid back than others and seldom seem to worry, while other people get worked up about the slightest thing? It has little to do with the situation they're faced with and everything to do with their response to it. Situations or cir-cumstances don't stress us out; we stress ourselves out by our response to the situations. And it is a choice. Two dif-ferent people could be faced with the exact same situation and have a different emotional response. Therefore they would experience different levels of stress. One might panic or worry, while the other stays calm. One might worry about the problem, while the other concentrates on a solution. One might have fear, while the other one has faith. Either way, it's a choice that we personally make. As you can see, it's a person's emotional response that causes stress. If we respond negatively, we will be more tense physically, but if we respond positively, we will be more relaxed. We will also deal more effectively with a situation and improve our chances of a more favorable outcome if we respond positively.

Negative emotions cause tension in our muscles, which in turn causes us to think more negative thoughts, resulting in a downward spiral. We might literally experience a pain in the neck, or anywhere else for that matter, as a result of negative emotions. The answer? Don't try and remedy the tension in your body directly. Forget about that and deal with the root cause: your emotions. Concentrate on eliminating the negative emotions; then you will eliminate the tension in your body. When your emotions are positive, your physical body will be relaxed and your overall wellbeing will improve.

You might have to backpedal even further to see what caused the negative emotions in the first place. It may be a destructive habit, or it could have been a certain negative action that caused you to experience negative emotions. In that case, you need to eliminate the behaviour in order to eliminate the emotions. Then you will be at peace. Remember, our ACTIONS cause EMOTIONS, which affect our physical WELLBEING. Get your actions right and your emotions will be right. Get your emotions right and your body will be right.

But never forget why you're working. Don't get so wrapped up in the "how to" of daily living that you lose sight of the "why." A slogan that's often used by achievers is "Work hard, Play hard." Balance is the key. One compliments the other. When they're working, they give 100 percent of their time and effort to their work, but when they're off, they're 100 percent off. They completely forget about work and focus only on rest and relaxation. If you want to get rid of stress, you need to master the art of being able to live only in the present moment; after all, the present is the only time there is!

for START!

The hardest part of anything is starting, don't you agree? Many people talk about great ideas and things they would like to do, but many never start. As a result, their dreams become a passing thought, and eventually they are forgotten. Sadly, many people fail to put their ideas into action and live the rest of their lives in mediocrity, never knowing what they could have achieved. Ideas are useless and dreaming is futile unless our ideas are acted upon. I've lost count of the amount of times I've heard people saying "If I ever win the lottery one day, I will do this or do that." Many of the people who I've heard saying that are now past sixty years of age and have been saying it for the last few decades. The problem is that nothing has changed and time is running out. But the real problem is that they have failed to start. They fail to realise that life is a game of choice, not chance. If you rely on winning the lottery to achieve your dreams, you will probably be extremely disappointed. Not only that, but think about all the wasted years that could have been spent taking action toward achieving your dreams. You could have used those years to start your own business or accomplish something great instead of waiting on something that will probably never happen and has about a fourteen million-to-one chance of happening.

Even if a person won the lottery when they were sixty

years of age, would it not have been better to become wealthy when they were thirty or forty instead? Then they would've had more time left to enjoy it. When you realise that life is a game of choice and not chance, you're more likely to start. When you take that first step toward pursuing your dreams, you're taking responsibility for creating your own destiny. But if you wait on winning the lottery in order to achieve your dreams, you've given away the control. You've allowed "chance" to determine whether you'll achieve your dreams or not. To me, that's not a recipe for success, it's a recipe for disappointment and failure. There are people who have become wealthy after a few years of hard work and persistent effort, yet there are people who have waited decades to win the lottery and are still waiting! All because they failed to start! I don't believe it's ever too late to do anything, but time is not on their side. We all have a limited amount of time on this planet, and tomorrow is not guaranteed. Why waste time? Statistics show that when a person does win the lottery, the money is usually gone in a relatively short period of time. Why? Because they got something for nothing. When you get something for nothing, you don't gain the strength of character required for success, and you don't learn any success principles. It's far better to become wealthy gradually, through your own efforts, than to get something for nothing. But the only way to do that is to start!

Have you ever noticed that the thought of doing something is actually worse than doing it? Once you've started, it's not half as bad as you thought. This is because our minds tend to multiply things and blow them out of proportion. But once we start, we often realise that the negative thoughts we had about it were false.

Some people fail to start because of fear. Others fail to start because they are lazy. Some people fail to start because they are waiting on the "right circumstances" and end up procrastinating. If fear is stopping you from starting, understand that your fear will increase the longer you put it off.

Only by taking action will you destroy fear. There is no other way.

If you are lazy, then there is nothing we can do for you. But I do not believe for a moment that you are lazy, or you wouldn't be reading this book just now. Just the fact that you've read this far shows that you're hungry enough to improve your life. It also puts you in the top five percent bracket in the country, because most people don't read these books. Well done for starting!

If you're waiting for the "right circumstances," understand that circumstances will never be "right" and you are likely to have a long wait. It reminds me of the man who wanted to drive from one side of the town to the other. He said, "I don't mind going as long as you can guarantee me that every set of traffic lights will be at green, I won't have to wait in any queues, there won't be any delays or hitchhikers, I won't get any punctures, I won't take any wrong turns, and the weather will be perfect." It's kind of ridiculous, isn't it? Because we all know life isn't like that. You need to start now, regardless of circumstances. You need to start where you are with what you've got.

When Hitler declared war on the United States in 1941, the U.S. Eighth Air Force began mounting daylight bombing raids over Germany. At first, the crews were unprepared for the kind of war they were getting into. Many had never seen combat before, but this didn't mean they didn't start. They started right away, with what they had, and learned as they went along. They suffered appalling losses to begin with, but this didn't stop the "Mighty Eighth." They were actually making up their own rules as they went along, which is the best way to learn. The best way to learn anything new is through trial and error. In the same way, this might mean adjusting your own strategy along the way, but at least you are moving. Instead of waiting for "right circumstances," why not create circumstances by taking action? Circumstances will never be "right." As you start, you might be surprised at how circumstances change, often in your favour, as a result of taking action. Someone once said, "Yesterday is a cancelled check, tomorrow is a promissory note, and today is a gift; that's why it's called "the present."

The dictionary defines the word "inertia" as "the feeling of unwillingness to do anything." In physics, Newton's first law of motion states that "An object at rest tends to stay at rest, and an object in motion tends to stay in motion, with the same speed and in the same direction, unless acted upon by an unbalanced force." In other words, objects tend to keep on doing what they're doing. This tendency to resist changes in their state of motion is described as inertia. But aren't many of our lives like that? We get so used to the same old routine week after week, month after month, year after year, that we resist new opportunities and we resist anything that involves change. This inertia can prevent us from making a start and achieving our dreams.

"An object at rest tends to stay at rest" could describe a lazy person, and "an object in motion tends to stay in motion with the same speed and in the same direction unless acted upon by an unbalanced force" could describe a person who gets into a rut and doesn't want to step outside their comfort zone, while the "unbalanced force" could mean redundancy or some other adverse situation which forces them to take action. But rather than wait to be acted upon by an "unbalanced force," why not start now while the going is good? You need to overcome inertia and develop some momentum. Once you've started, it's much easier to keep the momentum going. You could liken it to pushing a car. Once you've started pushing it, it's much easier to keep it going than it would be to stop, take a rest, and then start all over again. So, keep the momentum going. You might even want to increase it, but don't stop, or it will be much harder to start again. Starting also takes the most energy. When a rocket takes off, it uses eighty percent of its fuel to get a few feet off the ground. It then goes to the moon and back on the remaining twenty percent of its fuel. So why does it use so much fuel just to get a few feet off the ground? Because it has to overcome inertia. But once it's moving, it takes far less energy to keep it moving. By the same token, when something that has a large amount of mass is moving at high velocity, it's almost unstoppable because it has momentum.

Imagine for a moment a huge meteorite about a hundred feet wide, heading for planet earth at high velocity. Now that has momentum! How hard do you think it would be to stop it? Probably impossible. Now imagine the same meteorite at a standstill (after it has landed on the earth). How hard do you think it would be to get it moving? Almost impossible! Because now it has no momentum and has to overcome inertia. It's the same with us. If we sit around watching TV, the very thought of starting seems daunting, and it may take a great deal of willpower to get up and do something. But once we make a start and gain some momentum, we often become enthusiastic and don't want to stop. It's a psychological fact that motion creates emotion.

I was once told by a driving instructor that the most powerful gear on a car was not top gear, but first gear. He said that this is because it is the only gear that has to overcome inertia and move the car from a complete standstill. All the other gears, although they involve higher speeds, don't have to overcome inertia, because the car is already moving. Therefore, they are not as powerful as first gear. Procrastination is also something we need to overcome if we want to be successful. There is energy released in doing something now, but if we put things off, we tend to lose energy and become lethargic. Some people get caught up in the "someday syndrome." They might come up with a bunch of different things they would like to achieve but always seem to have an excuse for not starting. They might say things like, "Someday when I retire, I'm going to— ." Or, "If I ever win the lottery one day, I promise you I will— ." Or, "Once I get a raise or a promotion, I will— ," and it never gets done because they never start. The problem is that even if they do get a raise or a promotion, they find some other excuse instead.

It reminds me of the story of the man who promised his neighbour he would do some minor repairs on the bodywork of his car. He had been promising him for quite some time, but never seemed to get round to it. It was about the beginning of autumn when he first promised to do it. He said, "That's really a job for the better weather. If you can just wait until the winter is over I'll have a look at it." When spring came, the weather was still a bit changeable, and he said, "Once it gets a bit warmer I'll get it done. Summer is the ideal time for doing stuff like that." Two or three months later it was summer and it was really hot. He said, "My wife and I are going on holiday to Europe in a few weeks' time. I've got a lot to do between now and then and I don't want to rush the job. It would be better if I did it when I got back, and then I wouldn't have to rush it." Eventually he got back from his holiday and he said he just needed a bit of a rest because his wife had taken ill while they were away and the holiday was totally chaotic. He said he was also suffering from jet lag. By the time he felt better, the summer was coming to an end and the autumn was starting to creep in. He finally found the time to look at his neighbour's car and repaired it within a few hours. The extremely patient neighbour was delighted that it had eventually been done, but he thought that he might take it to a garage in the future. The moral of the story? If you don't want to do it then any excuse will do! But if you do want to do it, you will find a way and you will make the time. As someone wisely put it, "You can make excuses or you can make money; you can't do both."

But to do that, you need to start!

for TIME

Time is the most precious resource that we have. Every one of us, at this precise moment, has a certain amount of time left on this planet, and not one of us knows how long that will be. Time is more valuable than money. Money can be replaced, but time cannot. Time wasted is gone forever, and the clock is ticking. Time stands still for no man. The quality of your life depends on how you make use of your time. Every day when you get up, you choose what to do with your time. Some people spend their time wisely and use it for good purposes; others use it to plot evil. The thing we all have in common is that we all have free will and we are all responsible.

Everyone has twenty-four hours a day. Successful people have twenty-four hours a day and unsuccessful people have twenty-four hours a day. The difference is found in how they use their time. One person might go out to earn an honest day's living while another plans a terrorist attack on a massive scale. Yet both have twenty-four hours and both have a limited amount of time left. Some people are content to watch others achieve, while some want to achieve themselves. As a result, they will spend their time differently. Whether someone achieves greatly in life or whether they live a life of mediocrity has nothing to do with luck, as some might suggest, but has everything to do with how they spend their time.

Every day is a new beginning and an opportunity to begin again. The good news is, if you don't like where you're at, you can change course any time you want. But before choosing how to spend your time, you first need to know what you want. What do you want out of life? If time and money were unlimited, what would you do differently? Are you happy working for a boss, or would you prefer to have your own business? You've probably heard the saying, "Having your ladder up against the wrong wall," haven't you? Well, I believe there's also such a thing as having the wrong ladder. Imagine that the top of the wall is where your dreams are, and the ladder represents how you spend your time. Not every ladder will get you to the top of the wall; you need to have the right one. Some ladders lead to mediocrity, others lead to poverty, and some lead to financial freedom. If your dream is to be financially free, then working for a boss is the wrong ladder, because you will never be financially free working for a boss. You might like what you do and you might be making good money, but it is still the wrong ladder for financial freedom because you will never have time. But if mediocrity is your goal, then working for a boss could be the right ladder. It all depends on what you want. The goal must match up with the ladder.

One of the ladders to financial freedom is owning your own business. I say "one of the ladders" because there are many ladders to financial freedom. Investing is another such ladder (provided you know what you're doing!). But if financial freedom is your goal, then having your own business is a good start and is a ladder that can get you there. Whether you become financially free or not will be largely determined by whether you employ other people or not. If you operate as a one man business, your income depends solely on your own efforts; therefore you will never have time. If you don't go to work, you make no money. It's as simple as that. It's the time-money trap. But if you employ other people, you're leveraging your time through other people's efforts, and there is no limit to the amount of leverage you can have. This is one of the keys to great wealth; using other people's time. When you use other people's time, there is no limit to the amount of money you can make.

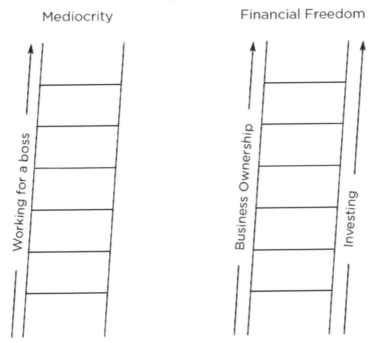

The financial freedom ladder makes use of
OPT (other people's time) and
OPM (other people's money)

Using other people's money is also a key to wealth, such as borrowing money for a down payment on a rental property. Remember, your bank manager is your friend. That's what he's there for. But, as previously mentioned, you need to be extremely careful before going into any kind of debt. As Robert Kiyosaki says, "If you're going to go into debt, make sure someone else is paying for it." Always remember the difference between good debt and bad debt.

People who base their future on utilising only their own time and their own money set themselves up for a lifestyle of "average," because their resources are limited. No matter how hard they work, they are limited by the amount of hours in a day, and there's usually a ceiling on what they can earn. This is especially true in the case of an employee. But take for example a business owner who employs 500 people. Suppose that each of these 500 people works eight hours a day. That's 4,000 hours of leverage (or productivity) per day!

Often this can enable the business owner to go on a cruise or be lying on some hot tropical beach while their business is still operating and producing income. In other words, they're making money and they have the time to go with it. That's the beauty of using other people's time!

Unfortunately for employees, they often work the hardest, are taxed the most, and sometimes have the least to show for it. Business owners, on the other hand, although many of them work hard, work smarter instead of harder (by using other people's resources). They have more tax advantages and usually have a better lifestyle (time and money freedom). But if you are an employee, why not start a business of your own? Even if it's a part-time business. You can then begin to leverage your time through other people's efforts. You can still keep your day job while building your own business and learning how to think like a business owner. Remember, you're only limited by your own thinking. Start thinking like a business owner, even if you're still working for a boss.

Another important aspect of success is "time management." Today more than ever before we are so busy running about here, there, and everywhere that it seems almost impossible to fit anything else into our schedule. But with some careful planning and discipline we can accomplish far more than we thought we could. It's just a case of managing our time. We can cut down on things that aren't important and allocate more time to things that are important. The first thing you need to do is prioritise. This means taking a good look at all the things that occupy your time on a daily basis and eliminating or cutting down on things that are non-productive and aren't going to contribute to your dreams.

For example, you may spend two or three hours in front of the TV every night and decide to cut it down to half an hour. You might be sitting in the coffee shop for two hours every day and decide to cut that down to half an hour. You might be spending too much time on the phone or too much time reading magazines, which you could be reduced considerably. There are probably many other areas that you can cut back in, if you really think about it. Once you've cut down or eliminated things that aren't going to contribute to your dreams, the next step is to put that time to good use. If, for example, you had your own part-time business, you could use that extra time to do more presentations. When you manage your time effectively, you will be amazed at the amount of things you can accomplish that you previously thought you never had time for. But the truth is, you do have the time! You've always had the time because you've always had twenty-four hours a day. It's just that you've chosen to spend your time differently. It's not a case of not having the time; it's a case of priorities. It's a case of saying yes to the important and no to the unimportant.

Of course there are still things you have to spend time doing that you may not want to do, such as buying groceries and doing chores around the house. But even these things can be allocated a certain slot of time that you can do at your own leisure. With the convenience of twenty-four-hour supermarkets, we can now fit in mundane things like shopping and household chores at a time of our choosing without allowing them to disrupt more important things, such as doing business presentations. Give high priority to the important and fit in the less important around the important. Personally, I would never waste time during the day or waste an evening doing shopping. During the day is for business (that is a priority), and evening is for business presentations (also a high priority). Shopping can be done any time and can be fitted in around these things. I often find myself shopping at eleven o'clock at night, sometimes later. But remember, success is not built on convenience; it's built on inconvenience, so you need to be flexible.

For example, you might decide that from 7:00 p.m. until 7:30 p.m. is for doing paperwork and making phone calls. Then you might have a business presentation at 8:30 p.m. This might mean that you miss your favourite TV program, but why not record it and watch it later on, after your presentation? Or you could use it as a reward for doing your next presentation. Remember, all work and no play makes Jack a dull boy. As busy as you are, there should always be a sensible balance between work and play. It is highly recommended that you use a diary or notebook to plan your schedule. Not only is it more professional, but it also disciplines you and stops you from forgetting. It also reduces stress because you don't have to "try" to remember.

For example, a person's schedule on a typical work day might look something like this:

WAKEN 6:30 a.m.: Listen to motivational CD while getting ready for and driving to work.

AT WORK 9:00 a.m.

LUNCHTIME 12:30-1:30 p.m. You could use this time to simply relax and have something to eat, or depending on your schedule you might want use this time to eat and read from a positive thinking book at the same time.

FINISH WORK 5:00 p.m. (back home for 6:00 p.m.) Use this time to listen to motivational CD while driving.

(6:00 p.m. - 7:00 p.m.) Have dinner, talk with family, etc.; relax. If you have chosen to stop watching TV, well done! Remember, negative news and programs do nothing for your emotional wellbeing and happiness. Why not have music on instead?

7:00 - 7:30 p.m.   Phone calls / paperwork, etc.

8:30 p.m. Business presentation.   (Listen to favourite music while driving)   Remember, it's not all about motivational input. There also has to be a time when we psychologically switch off from work and listen to music. (Or maybe even silence?)

10:30 p.m. Back home. Quality time with spouse. Nothing gets to interrupt this time! It is well deserved. You may choose to not even answer the phone and simply let it go to voicemail.

Now that's just an example, and you how you plan your schedule is up to you. Remember, there's a big difference between being busy and being productive. Everyone is busy, but not everyone is productive. For example, someone might spend all day doing things like washing dishes, mowing the lawn, cleaning out the garage, rearranging the furniture, and having coffee, but nothing has been accomplished in terms of taking them closer to their dreams. So remember to prioritise. Your time is valuable, so don't waste it.

Last but not least, we need to remember to respect other people's time. Their time is just as valuable as ours. If you have an appointment with someone, make sure you are on time. This applies to anything, not just business. By being on time you're showing respect for the other person and it also helps to discipline you. Why not make a habit of arriving ten or fifteen minutes early? Then you will arrive in a relaxed state of mind instead of being stressed out. You can then use this extra time to sit in your car, gather your thoughts, and plan what you're going to say, rather than simply be focusing on getting there on time. It could make all the difference to the results you get. I remember times when I had presentations booked and I was in such a rush to get there that my whole focus on the way there was about getting there on time rather than focusing on what I would say at the presentation and what I wanted to achieve. Instead of thinking about the reason I was doing it, I was watching the clock. As a result, when I got there I was stressed out and I wasn't as mentally prepared as I should have been. Maybe my presentation wasn't as good either? But had I left a little earlier to get there, I wouldn't have been so concerned about being late or rushing to get there. Instead, I could have used that whole journey to focus on that I wanted to achieve, and also used it as a time for some mental relaxation by listening to my favourite music. Then I would have arrived in a more positive state of mind and my focus would have been on the right things. If we use our time wisely and don't leave things until the last minute, we will reduce our stress considerably.

for UNDERSTAND

Someone once said that nothing in life is to be feared, it is only to be understood. We need to realise that fear is largely based on ignorance. When we are faced with unknown situations or doing something we've never done before, we can often be our own worst enemies by imagining the worst possible things happening. The less we know about something, the more fear we have. This is because we don't know the facts. When we know the facts, we can focus on the facts, but when we don't know the facts, we have nothing to focus on. This is when our imagination kicks in and results in causing fear.

The more knowledge we have of something, the less fear we have, but the irony of the whole situation is that we first have to face what we fear before we can gain knowledge. This calls for courage; for it is only through experiencing something that we truly understand. We can get people's advice about certain things or we can read about them, but neither of these things will ever be a substitute for experience. I once heard a saying which I thought was very true:

> I hear and I forget
> I see and I remember
> I do and I understand

This is also proof of the fact that our brain absorbs some things more readily through some of the five senses than others. Of all the five senses, our eyes, by far, retain the highest percentage of information. For example, if someone is trying to explain something to us and tells us without showing us, it's easily forgotten because we may not fully understand. If someone tells us something and we take notes, we have a higher chance of remembering it because it went in through our eyes as well as our ears. If someone explains something using pictures or a flipchart, we are far more likely to remember. We retain a much higher percentage of what we see compared to what we hear because we think in pictures, not in words. But only when we do something do we fully understand. When we do something, we also engage our sense of touch. The more senses involved, the bigger the impression it makes on the subconscious mind. For example, if you wanted to learn how to drive a car, how successful do you think you would be if you never took any lessons, but instead you got in the car with your driving instructor and he did the driving all the time? You were never allowed to experience driving the car; all you were allowed to do was to sit in the passenger seat, ask questions, and listen to his advice. Do you think you would understand what to do? Not nearly as well as you would by actually doing it.

What do you think would happen if suddenly he put you in for your test after a few months of doing this? Would you feel confident? Do you think you would understand what to do? I highly doubt it, because although we learn a lot by seeing and hearing, no amount of seeing and hearing will ever be a substitute for "doing." For it's only in the "doing" that we fully understand. It's only in the "doing" that we gain confidence. It's only in the "doing" that we make mistakes and learn to correct them. It's only in the "doing" that we form habits.

I remember one time when my car wouldn't start. I was parked outside a shop because I'd been doing some work for the owner. I didn't know what was wrong with it, so he came out, lifted up the bonnet, fiddled about with a few things, and within a few minutes got it started. I was obviously overjoyed that he had managed to start it. So I thanked him and said, "What did you do?" And he simply said, "Aha!" and wouldn't tell me. I asked him again and he said, "One of the tricks of the trade." I was extremely grateful, but at the same time I was never going to understand. If he had shown me what to do I could have learned what to do if a similar situation arose in the future. Not only that, but when we understand something we can also pass our knowledge on to other people and help them to understand.

HOW WE RETAIN INFORMATION

83%	by	Sight
11%	by	Hearing
3.5%	by	Smell
1.5%	by	Touch
1%	by	Taste

Confusion is the opposite of understanding. Sometimes we're in the middle of a struggle or an emotional battle and we aren't sure which way to go or why certain things are happening to us, and we're confused. At times like that we're called on to have faith. We need to have faith that God is helping us and guiding us because He is. The Bible tells us, "I will instruct you and teach you in the way you should go, I will counsel you and watch over you." (Psalm 32:8).

If we have the courage to persist, God will make things clearer to us as we go along. Then gradually we will begin to understand. We must never forget that God is our Ultimate Counsellor and wants us to succeed. God guides us and instructs us in the most unexpected ways. Sometimes God works through other people to get the advice to us, but I must also make it clear that I am not talking about visiting mediums or fortune tellers and the like. All these things are condemned in the Bible because we end up putting our faith in them instead of God. Things like that will actually take you away from God. It is far better to take our requests to God in prayer than to turn to a medium or a fortune teller. But even then, we still need to be extremely careful of who we take advice from, because there are times when I've been given the wrong advice and it got me even deeper into the mess I was already in. So how do we know if it's good advice? Well, I can only speak from my own experience, but when I was given wrong advice, it was not Bible-based advice. I'm sure the person meant well, but through sheer ignorance it was not good advice. I later spoke to a good Christian friend who gave me the exact opposite advice, which was Bible-based advice. This led to my problem being solved and a breakthrough to a new level of success. It also led to a whole new understanding on my part and a deeper desire to understand the Bible. Never forget that the Bible is the Truth and will help us not only in our quest for success, but also in helping us to understand any situation life throws at us.

God also speaks to us through the books we read. But before I go any further, I won't be foolish enough to try and limit God to the ways in which He counsels us by attempting to list them here. I'm merely giving some examples because His ways are limitless and beyond our understanding. I've lost count of the amount of times I've asked for guidance and a short time later read something in a book that answered my question for me. It's happened too many times to be coincidence, and it always seems to happen at just the right time. "Ask and it will be given to you; seek and you will find." (Matt 7:7).

When you're in the midst of your struggles, realise that with persistence will come understanding. If you quit, you'll never understand because the opportunity will be gone, but as long as you persist you'll eventually succeed and you'll understand. I'm not a mathematician, but these two formulas have proved themselves to be true time and time again:

CONFUSION + PERSISTENCE = UNDERSTANDING

TRAGEDY + TIME = HUMOUR

I must be completely honest with you; in the past I've been guilty of blaming God for some of my struggles. I honestly thought He was punishing me for something. But as time went by, it gradually became clear to me that I was the cause of my own struggles, not God. It became evident to me that the emotional pain I was in was due to some of my own negative habits. I had absolutely no idea that this was caused by my own doing, and here I was blaming the Almighty! I later came across a verse in the Bible that said, "A man's own folly ruins his life, yet his heart rages against the Lord." (Prov 19:3) I think God was trying to tell me something!

I began to think back to other previous struggles, and mentally examined each one. In every case I could see how I myself had unknowingly created them through negative habits. I realised that it was time to take responsibility for my life to and stop blaming God. God wasn't punishing me; he was merely bringing them to my attention so that I could get out of them. It was time to realise that God wants us to succeed, not fail. He also wants us to understand. This calls for courage, because in order to understand we need to face our fears. Realise that a lack of understanding can always be traced back to a lack of knowledge. The solution? Get knowledge! Start reading a little bit every day.

"Wisdom is supreme; therefore get wisdom. Though it cost all you have, get understanding." (Prov 4:7).

A lack of understanding can also lead to failure. This can be seen in all types of situations, ranging from war to business. The book of Proverbs says, "Plans fail for lack of counsel, but with many advisors they succeed." (Prov 15:22) From what I've observed, particularly in network market-ing, the people who failed (gave up) were, in the vast majority of cases, people who wouldn't listen to advice. They simply wouldn't listen to people who were more successful than they were, even though these people had "the fruit on the tree." They were either too stubborn, had too much "status," or simply thought they knew best. As a result, they didn't understand what they needed to know and ended up failing. Many people look upon it as a weakness to ask for advice and admit they don't understand something, but it's actually a strength. It's a weakness not to have the guts to do it.

In war, military commanders need to understand what's happening on the front line in order to make wise decisions. If they didn't understand the truth about the situation, they wouldn't be able to make wise decisions, because they would be making their decisions based on falsehood instead of reality. As a result, they would fail. One of the reasons Hitler lost the war is because he wouldn't listen to advice from his own men, and no one dared to tell him bad news for fear of being punished. When German cities were being subjected to "'round the clock bombing" in the later years of the war, the Germans had introduced a new jet fighter (Me 262) that was capable of ripping the Allied bombers apart.

But Hitler didn't want it used against the bombers; he wanted it used against the advancing land armies. The Luftwaffe protested because they understood the situation. They knew that this jet fighter could help save German cities from saturation bombing. But Hitler refused. Hitler's decision sentenced the German cities to rubble.

Another important part of understanding is under-standing how other people tick. Not only that, but also un-derstanding how we ourselves tick. It stands us in good stead when dealing with other people. Whatever we project to-ward other people we will get back in return. If we project friendliness we are likely to receive friendliness. If we project hostility we are likely to receive hostility. Therefore we literally set the tone by what we project, almost like a thermostat setting the temperature in a room. With a thermostat, if the temperature in the room is too hot or too cold, we simply adjust the thermostat and we will get a different result in terms of temperature. In a similar way, if we don't like the results we're getting from other people, it could be that we have our "relational thermostat" set wrong. It could be that we're subconsciously projecting the wrong things such as a negative attitude, hostility, or intolerance. In that case, we need to change our "relational thermostat" to one of projecting friendliness, sincerity, and understanding instead. When you change, the results also change, but it all starts with you. You are the "thermostat."

To effectively deal with people, it's essential to understand this basic law. People also like us or dislike us according to how we make them feel emotionally. Every time we talk to someone, it has some kind of emotional effect on them. We either leave them feeling better or worse for having spoken to us. Choose the former. For example, if you were walking past your neighbour's house and they were outside painting their fence, you could say one of two things. You could tell them what a great job they were doing and how much better the fence looked, or you could tell them that the weather forecast was terrible and it would probably be raining shortly. Two different comments causing two different types of emotions. One made them happy, the other not so happy. Telling them it's going to rain soon isn't going to cheer them up, so why say it? In fact, if you make them feel bad, they'll probably wish they'd never clapped eyes on you.

You might be thinking, "But that's the truth. I've heard the forecast." Well it might be the forecast, but is it absolutely necessary to say it? In this case, it's not absolutely necessary to say it.

If it starts to rain, they'll soon notice all by themselves. They don't need you to tell them. When you're talking to people, make it a habit to actually go out of your way to look for things to compliment. Go out of your way to make people feel good.

It's all about what you focus on. The person who tells them it's going to rain soon is focusing on negative things. The person who compliments them is focusing on positive things. If you can't think of anything good to say, don't say anything at all, unless it's absolutely necessary.

UNDERSTANDING HUMAN NATURE

When you're talking with someone, your focus should always be on them and not on yourself. You can't do both at the same time. Forget about yourself while you're talking to them. In the fore- front of your mind should always be things like, "How are they getting on?" "What's going on in their life?" "What questions can I ask?" "What's important to them?" "What hobbies and interests do they have?" "What things can I sincerely compliment?" "How can I encourage them and build them up?" "How can I leave them feeling better for have spoken to me?"

If you make a habit of operating this way and asking questions such as these, you will win many friends and you will be well liked. Keep the focus on them. If they are talking about their holiday and you have also been on holi- day, don't feel the need to tell them about your holiday unless they ask you. Because what you are doing is shifting the focus from them, back onto yourself. Never do that! This is a major mistake that many people make, and is not a sign of being a good conversationalist. Resist the urge to talk about yourself. Instead, ask them another question. You should be able to talk at length with someone, from start to finish, without ever having mentioned yourself. You should be content to walk away from a conversation without them ever having asked you a question. By all means, if they ask you something, tell them. You don't want to give the im- pression of being secretive or being like a closed book ei- ther, but as soon as you have answered, switch the focus back onto them. When you understand how to control con- versations and begin to take a sincere interest in people, people will be drawn to you like a magnet.

for VISUALISE

"If you can dream it, you can do it."
(Walt Disney)

Walt Disney had a vision of Disneyland long before it became a reality. Before something is created physically, it first has to be created mentally. This takes place in the imagination. Walt Disney had a rule that whenever he had an idea, he would bring at least ten of his advisors into a room and bounce the idea off them. If at least nine of them didn't think he was crazy he would throw away the idea— which proves that if you want to be successful, you can't be thinking like the masses.

Successful people know that if you want succeed, you've got to expect criticism and ridicule. So expect criticism. Welcome it. It simply means you're on the right track. Bruce Lee said "There are no limits except the limits you place on yourself." Someone once said, "Whatever the mind of man can conceive and believe, it can achieve." Which is very true, but we have to believe. To achieve something, you first need to believe it is possible. Jesus said, "Everything is possible for him who believes." (Mark 9:23) Notice how Jesus didn't say "some things;" He said, "Everything," and Jesus only speaks the truth.

Visualisation isn't something that is reserved only for great achievers and inventors and the like; we all use visualisation every day. Most of us are probably not even aware that we are visualising things. We visualise outcomes to situations we are faced with. We visualise ourselves succeeding, or we visualise ourselves failing. We visualise things going right, or we visualise things going wrong. But the point is, we visualise something. When you are faced with a tough situation, do you visualise things going right or do you visualise them going wrong? Whatever you picture in your imagination most often is what your subconscious accepts as "the goal" and is what you will attract. As Maxwell Maltz explains in his bestselling book Psycho Cybernetics, our subconscious mind is a goal-seeking mechanism which is always striving to achieve something. Maltz explains that the mental images we hold in our imagination are the "goals" for our subconscious to work upon. If you picture yourself failing most of the time, you are likely to fail. But if you picture yourself succeeding most of the time, then you are likely to succeed. The subconscious simply cannot act any other way except upon the information we feed it. This also includes the words we speak, which is covered in the next chapter.

Always picture yourself succeeding and performing exactly as you want to perform. We literally determine what we become, by what we repeatedly picture in our imagination most often. If you constantly picture yourself as inferior, you will keep yourself locked in a self imposed cycle of negativity. But if you picture yourself succeeding and coming out on top in everything you do, you will program yourself to do just that.

Just as we need to picture in our minds what we want to happen, we also need to be speaking positive words (what we want to happen). One of the most famous inventors of all time, Thomas Edison, used his imagination while "sitting for ideas." He found that he got his best ideas when he was in a drowsy state, almost ready to fall asleep. He also said that ideas are "in the air," and that if he hadn't thought of it, someone else would have, which leads us to think, how many unthought-of ideas are there? They are probably infinite; that's why we haven't thought of them! Yet we limit ourselves by saying things like, "I can't think of anything else," or, "That's as far as I can go," and we cut ourselves off from future possibilities. If you cut yourself off mentally, you will cut yourself off physically. It's not that the possibilities aren't there; we simply turn our backs on them by refusing to believe they are there. It's only by believing something is possible that break-throughs are made. Richard Branson, Alexander Bell, Neil Armstrong, Henry Ford, and the Wright Brothers all bear testimony to that. All of them started with a vision of what could be possible and took action, regardless of what the critics said or what odds they were up against.

Visualising is being able to see with your mind what you can't see with your eyes. But before I go any further, I am not talking about some paranormal or occult behaviour, I'm simply meaning being able to see in your imagination a desired possible outcome before it even exists. For example, a painter visualises a finished painting before he even picks up a brush. An author visualises their book being read by millions of people even before it's published. An athlete visualises himself winning a race long before the race even takes place. All the time they are training, they are visualising themselves being first across the finish line. In other words, they see with their mind what they cannot see with their eyes. Is it egotism? Certainly not! It's simply positive thinking at its best. What they are doing is setting a very definite goal for the subconscious mind.

Let's face it, there are only two things you can picture: success or failure. If you don't picture success then you automatically picture failure. Even as I write this book I am visualising it being read by millions of people and helping them to change their lives for the better. Never go into anything visualising defeat. While we may occasionally experience defeat, it should never be because we ourselves created it by visualising it.

Visualising a positive outcome is the opposite of worrying. Ironically, both work in the exact same way, only the
goal is different. Visualisation involves picturing in your
mind what you want to happen, while worrying involves
picturing what you don't want to happen. In both cases it's
acted upon as a "goal." Many people have used visualisation
to recover from serious illnesses. Instead of mentally accepting that they were ill (providing their subconscious with
a negative goal), they continually pictured themselves in
excellent health and spoke words of health, thus providing
positive mental images for their subconscious to act upon.
They visualised the good cells in their blood destroying the
foreign particles. Eventually through repetition, the subconscious began to accept this new picture and acted upon it.
In many cases a recovery was made.

But unfortunately visualisation is not always used
positively. Some people use visualisation negatively and
hold a negative mental image of themselves. For example,
some people have a fear of getting old. The reason they are
afraid is because the mental image they have of themselves
in their later years is one of poor health, poverty, and possibly being unable to fend for themselves. Some of them
even talk about some day ending up in a retirement home.
My question is, "What kind of goal have they set for themselves?" Obviously it is an extremely negative one. Many of
them have been thinking this way for many years and the
thought is now firmly embedded in their subconscious
mind. They are probably unaware that they have provided
their subconscious with a very vivid and definite goal.

Have you ever noticed some of the road signs warning
drivers to approach with caution because there are elderly
people about? The one I remember has a symbol of two old
people stooped over, almost hunchbacked, with walking
sticks. And underneath, the words, "Elderly People." I
thought to myself, isn't this typical of the kind of stereo-
typing (some might say brainwashing) that society expects
us to accept and conform to? If we accept this as a picture of

how we can expect to be in our later years, then we have just provided our subconscious mind with this goal. But you don't have to accept this. You can, if you wish, reject this thought and refuse to accept this as a "goal." You can, if you wish, continue to picture yourself as still being young. A major key to this picture is how you act. How you act sends a very powerful and definite message to your subconscious, telling it what sort of person you are. If you continue to act young and refuse to let "age" influence your behaviour, then your subconscious will still hold a picture of you as being young, and as a result, you will feel young. But if you allow "age" to dictate to you what you can and can't do, and act as an old person, your subconscious will hold a picture of you as being old, and you will begin to feel old. In either case, your THOUGHTS lead to ACTIONS, which determine how you FEEL, which in turn affect your LOOKS. (Remember, your emotions affect your body.)

I know people who are in their sixties and still go horse riding and live very active lives. I know people in their seventies who still look as fit and healthy as people half their age. They have not allowed society or "age" to influence their behaviour. They still have a positive mental picture of themselves, and quite rightly so. Remember;

"No one is as old as the person who stops having fun." (Henry David Thoreau)

Visualisation can be used to improve any aspect of your life. For example, you might want to use it to improve your public speaking abilities. If you were to stand in front of an audience right now of a hundred or so people and give a talk, how would you feel? What kind of picture would you have of yourself? Would it be one of confidence and poise or would it be one of fear and failure? Would you picture yourself delivering a good talk or would you picture yourself making mistakes and embarrassing yourself?

Your answer to these questions is what your subconscious acts upon and brings about. But the good news is that if you have a negative picture of yourself failing, you can change the picture. Through practice and repetition, you can change the picture to a positive, successful one. Isn't that good news? That's why I don't believe anyone is a failure, because everyone has the ability to change by changing the picture they have of themselves. If someone believes they are a failure, it's simply because they've accepted a false picture of themselves. It's virtually impossible to act inconsistently with the picture we have of ourselves.

So how do we change the picture? We do it by repeatedly acting "as if" we are the type of person we want to become. If we are lacking confidence, we act as if we are confident. The subconscious cannot tell the difference between a real experience and one which is vividly imagined. Therefore, if we vividly imagine ourselves as being confident and acting confidently, our subconscious responds emotionally, as if it were really happening, and this becomes the "goal" for our subconscious to act upon. The more often we do it, the more definite it becomes, and the more it gets impressed on our subconscious mind.

But don't wait until you're in a real-life situation to practice; the key is to practice in privacy, without the pressure of a real situation. If, for example, you were to practice giving a talk to an imaginary group of people in the privacy of your own room, and you were to imagine it in great detail, your subconscious would think an actual event had taken place. You would create the same mental images as you would have in a real situation. Then, when a real situation comes along, your subconscious calls on these images and acts accordingly. In short, you would have "tricked" your subconscious into succeeding. You would also experience the positive emotions and feelings of success that go along with it. Emotions and feelings are very important because they are the keys to making a powerful impression on the subconscious. The more emotion, the bigger the impact. Your conscious mind knows it was imaginary, but the subconscious doesn't. We can actually "fool" the subconscious into success, just as we can "fool'" it into failure. You would probably feel more confident giving a talk to an imaginary group of people than you would giving a talk to a real live audience. But here's what eventually happens: every time you practice talking to this imaginary group, you're programming your subconscious with this "feeling of confidence." Through constant practice and repetition, you begin to bombard the subconscious with this "feeling of confidence" which will override and replace the old feelings of failure you had of yourself.

You are actually programming it with a new picture of you; a confident and successful picture instead of a failure picture. Don't worry if you don't feel successful just now. Do it anyway and the subconscious will gradually start to accept the new picture. I once read that "normal conditions can be restored with greater ease and certainty than abnormal conditions can be induced." Notice how it says "restored," meaning that it was yours to begin with. You were not born with an image of failure. Unfortunately, somewhere along the road of life you developed a negative self concept. A concept which is false and needs to be replaced with the truth.

When you give a talk to an imaginary group of people, three things are vital: Firstly, it has to be done frequently and for at least thirty days to profoundly affect your self-image. I would recommend twice a day, first thing in the morning and last thing at night, in order to get the subconscious to accept the new picture of you. Secondly, you need to imagine it in as much detail as possible, making it more "real" to your subconscious mind. The more real it seems, the more readily it will be accepted by your subconscious mind. Thirdly, you must "see yourself" performing well. You must be acting exactly as you wish to be in real life. If you want to be confident, you must be acting confidently when speaking to this imaginary group.

When you have done this often enough, the next time you are faced with a real live audience, these imaginary experiences are called on by your subconscious, and the feelings of confidence and poise that accompanied them "carry over" into your real life situation. Your subconscious acts exactly how you have programmed it and it acts the same with the real audience as it did with the imaginary audience. Remember, it doesn't know the difference.

How you program it in practice is how it will "act" in reality.

MAKE IT REAL

In order to make the maximum impact on your subconscious, these imaginary experiences should be as realistic and vivid as possible. This technique can be applied to any aspect of your life that you wish to improve, but to keep things simple I will use the example of public speaking. When you are doing this make sure there are no distractions such as music, children, pets, TV, telephone, etc. The idea is to make it as real as possible, and I doubt any of these things would be present at a real live presentation.

If you would normally use a flipchart during a real presentation, use one in the privacy of your own room. If you would normally wear a suit and tie, wear a suit and tie in your own room. Some people have even been known to lay out rows of empty chairs when giving an imaginary talk because they found it much easier to visualise an audience sitting there. When you are talking, give full concentration to what you are doing and actually say the words out loud. Don't worry if people think you're crazy; the payoff will be worth it! When you're talking, use your imagination to picture yourself doing well. Picture rows and rows of people smiling and nodding and being very receptive to your talk. Picture everything going exactly as you want it to. You could even picture someone introducing you at the beginning of the talk, where you speak the words out loud, pretending to be the other person, and your audience cheering and clapping at the end, at which point you could thank them (out loud of course!). It's up to you how you do it, as long as it feels real to you. Incidentally, if you actually clap, it will have a very powerful effect on your subconscious and seem very real.

Visualisation can also be used to help us break negative habits as well as create positive ones. I remember the story of a man who used visualisation to help him stop biting his nails. He had tried "consciously" many times to stop, but to no avail. He had tried consciously (using willpower), but realised this was doing it the hard way and seldom worked. He decided it was better to utilise the power of the mighty subconscious, by using visualisation rather than willpower. This technique was effortless, but more effective.

So he decided to try a different approach. Every time he went to bite his nails he would hold a picture in his imagination of what his nails might look like under a microscope. He imagined them as black and dirty, crawling with millions of germs. The very thought of this almost made him sick. After a few weeks of doing this, the thought of horrible, dirty black nails began to pop into his mind automatically whenever he went to bite his nails. As soon as his fingers touched his mouth, he would visualise millions of black germs ready to leap from his dirty nails onto his tongue and down his throat and into his stomach. This began to act as a "trigger" for him to correct his behaviour. Through repetition, the subconscious had made a connection between biting his nails and something repulsive. After practicing this technique for several weeks, he eventually had no desire to bite his nails anymore because the thought of it "made him sick." No conscious effort was required, only imagination. Remember, imagination is very powerful, so use it to your advantage. Always picture what you want to happen, not what you fear might happen.

for WORDS

In the last chapter we spoke about how visualisation can help us change the picture we have of ourselves. But words also have creative power. When you say something, you create it. Words are very powerful and will change, override, or alter the mental images we hold in our minds. Words give direction to our subconscious mind. This is exactly what affirmations are all about; changing the programming in our subconscious mind and changing the direction in which we want it to go. The dictionary defines the word "affirm" as "declare to be true" or "uphold or confirm" (an idea or belief). An affirmation means saying out loud to yourself whatever you want to be true, regardless of what you feel is true. This alone is good news for anyone who has a negative self image and wants to change the picture they have of themselves. A different picture will mean realising and developing the potential which is already there. Some people may not believe it's there, but it's there. A different picture could mean becoming more outgoing and overcoming shyness. It could mean developing more self confidence. It could simply mean seeing yourself succeeding instead of failing, or whatever. If you don't believe you have the potential to become better than you are just now, then that is exactly where the problem lies; your beliefs are false. But beliefs can be changed, especially if they're based on falsehood. If you tell yourself something often enough, eventually you will start to believe it.

Everyone has the potential to become whatever kind of person they want if, and only if, they feed their subconscious mind the appropriate information. For example, you will not become more self confident by telling yourself that you aren't good at this and aren't good at that. You will not become a good public speaker if you tell yourself you aren't good at speaking in public or that you hate having to stand in front of an audience and talk. That is programming yourself to fail. Words like that create an image of failure in your mind. Only by speaking words of success and by saying what you want will you break out of the cycle of failure. If you want to develop self confidence, you need to tell your-self, "I am confident" (In the present tense), instead of saying, "I am not good at this and not good at that." If you want to become a good public speaker, you need to firstly tell yourself you are an excellent public speaker, and sec-ondly, you need to learn to like it. Notice how both things are positive (saying what you want). But you might be thinking, hold on a minute, I don't like speaking in public and I really don't think I'm excellent at it. Yes, that may be true at the moment, but it doesn't have to stay that way. Forget about what you're like just now. If it's not positive, wipe it out. You need to start focusing on what you want, not what you feel is true just now. You need to start focusing on the future instead of the past. Unless you stop repeating negative statements like that and start saying what you want, you will never become better. Focus only on what you want!

If you don't like speaking in public, is that what you really want to be true? If the answer is no, then stop saying it and start saying what you really want. I'm sure if we're really honest with ourselves, we all want to be good at it and we all want to like it. The reason most of us don't like it is because we feel we aren't good at it, and we have a fear of it. So if you say you don't like public speaking, your subcon-scious will probably have the sneaking suspicion that you're telling yourself you're not good at it, and you will continue to program yourself to fail. A lot of the programming the subconscious receives is the hidden, indirect messages behind some of the things we say, and these are just as powerful. If you say you don't like something, your subconscious knows the reason behind it.

The mental images you have of yourself will always be subservient to the words you speak, not the other way about. Therefore, you have a very powerful tool at your disposal (the tongue), and you can literally speak into existence the kind of person you want to become. When you speak words, they immediately affect your state of mind and become real. Affirmations are the goals we set for our subconscious to act upon and bring into actual physical reality, regardless of any evidence to the contrary.

Regardless of our past conditioning and previous experiences, we can change the picture we have of ourselves. Affirmations must always be stated positively and in the present tense. There's no point in stating it in the future because tomorrow never comes, and it is likely to stay in the future. So if you want to become confident, say "I AM CONFIDENT" (now).

I recommend doing this at least twice a day (minimum). First thing in the morning and last thing at night are preferable. You might even want to set aside specific times of day for using affirmations, but anytime is suitable. Do this until you get to a point where you actually feel confident and you no longer have to think about it anymore. In other words, do it until your subconscious has accepted it and it has become part of your psyche. What actually happens is that subconsciously, your behaviour will change. About ninety percent of our behaviour is subconscious. The words you speak program your subconscious. Your subconscious controls your habitual behaviour, and because your subconscious has been programmed differently (by using different words), it acts differently. In other words:

DIFFERENT WORDS $\longrightarrow$ DIFFERENT BEHAVIOR
DIFFERENT BEHAVIOR $\rightarrow$ DIFFERENT RESULTS
DIFFERENT RESULTS $\longrightarrow$ DIFFERENT SELF IMAGE

Your subconscious cannot help but act differently as a result of being programmed differently. It has no choice and will act exactly as you tell it. Unfortunately, some people use words that keep them locked into a life of failure and limitation. Through sheer ignorance they don't realise the power of words and they don't realise the damage they are doing to themselves. If, for example, a person had tried speaking in public and performed badly, they might say something like, "I'm terrible at public speaking," and they repeat these words often. Instead of saying what they want, they say what they don't want, and that is exactly what they get. Their subconscious responds by saying, "Okay, since I control ninety percent of your behaviour, I'll see to it that you are a terrible public speaker. The next time you try it, if you ever try again, I'll make sure you perform very badly." And as long as they're saying that, they always will be bad. On the other hand, if they were to say, "I'm an excellent public speaker," (even if they felt it wasn't true), their sub-conscious would respond by saying, "Okay, I realise you're not excellent just now, but as long as you keep saying that, I'll keep improving your behaviour until you do become excellent at it."

So, what is the answer? The answer is that they need to do something to break out of the negative cycle of failure. But people who have a deep-rooted picture of failure and a poor self image might have a hard time seeing themselves performing well, even in an imaginary situation. This is where affirmations come in. This is where they need to be completely honest with themselves and identify the areas they feel weak in and would like to change. Only when they have identified their weaknesses can they find a solution. For example, if they lack confidence and suffer from an inferiority complex, they need to affirm the opposite. They could say, "I am a confident, outgoing person. I am as good as anyone else." This is the key to making affirmations work and how to change your self image. First, identify the problem, being brutally honest with yourself, and then affirm the opposite (which is what you want). Do this in as many areas of your life as you feel necessary and would like to change. Different areas could include self image; financial, physical, spiritual, and emotional. I've included some examples of affirmations later in this chapter.

Affirmations will smash the vicious cycle of failure and help you break out of the chains you are in. Affirmations will put you into a positive cycle of success. Affirmations are the bridge from failure to success. Affirmations are the key to changing the picture you have of yourself. So why not free yourself from all these unnecessary restrictions and become the person God intended you to be? To be free physically you first need to be free mentally. To live an unlimited life you need to get rid of unnecessary limits. There's such a thing as a straight jacket, but I believe there's also such a thing as a psychological straight jacket. It's worn by people who live their lives with so many self-imposed limitations that they live extremely restricted and shallow lives. These restrictions are not real but imaginary, and have been fabricated in the workshop of their own minds. This is usually a result of past negative experiences or previous failures. Unfortunately, many people believe that these limitations are true, and they cause people to deny themselves the success they deserve. But this doesn't have to be the case.

The Bible says, "The tongue has the power of life and death." (Prov 18:21) Life and death are the two most opposite extremes that exist, so it stands to reason that if both of these extremes are affected by your words, then everything else in between these two extremes must also be affected. That means your happiness, your emotional state, your health, your finances, your relationships, EVERYTHING! This means you can also create either health or illness by the words you speak. Unfortunately some people think about illness, speak about illness, expect illness, and get illness. Is it any surprise? Not really, because they have provided their subconscious with a very definite and negative goal. How else is it supposed to respond?

If someone doesn't feel well, often they will say they don't feel very well (saying what they don't want), but they could, on the other hand, tell themselves they're getting better and better (what they want). They could, if they so desired, tell themselves they feel great, even if they don't. By doing this, they would be providing their subconscious with a picture of health, rather than simply accepting a negative goal of illness. Obviously our emotions also play a major part in our well being, but the ironic thing is that people who speak positive words usually have a more positive emotional state, and people who speak negative words usually have a negative emotional state. In both cases, their words have helped to create it. This only confirms that our brains are programmed by the words we speak. Your WORDS create EMOTIONS which affect your BODY.

When you are in close proximity with someone who is ill, it's not so much the fact that you're in contact with them that determines whether you catch something or not, but it has more to do with your words, your emotional state (which is linked to your immune system), your level of belief, and what you expect. For example, many people, after being in close contact with someone who is ill, expect to get ill, talk about getting ill, focus on it, and create a negative emotional state of worry and fear. As a result, they catch it but don't realise that they themselves created it. Bugs and germs are around us all the time and are just waiting for a gap in our defenses so they can get at us. Positive emotions strengthen our immune system, while negative emotions weaken it and drain our energy. When we speak words, we generate either positive or negative emotions. Although the actual words may only last a few seconds, the emotion that accompanied them will last for the whole day because emotion is subconscious. That's why a burst of anger can totally spoil the rest of your day, even after the event is over. On the other hand, if you were to speak only positive uplifting words, you would feel much happier as a result. Our emotions accumulate on a moment-to-moment and day-to-day basis, based on the words we habitually speak.

Most people are actually unaware that they are creating their future by the words they speak. Bestselling author Robert Kiyosaki often says in his books that there are words which make you rich and words which make you poor. We spoke in the last chapter about people who have a fear of getting old. Some people talk about being "too old" to do certain things, and they say it frequently. Remember that our actions as well as our words help to create the picture we have of ourselves, but because the two are so closely intertwined, I thought I should mention it here. I think retirement plays a huge part in the ageing process, but people don't just retire (actions), they also talk about it (words). Often they talk about retiring a long time before it happens (sometimes years before it happens). This firmly establishes the goal in their subconscious mind by making it vivid and definite (which also includes a date). When they do actually retire, they talk about it regularly by saying things like, "Now that I've retired, I will— ," or "Now that I've retired, I will have time to do—."

In other words, over the course of many years they have provided a very definite picture of themselves to their subconscious mind. But the important thing to realise is this: It's not so much retirement itself, but the mental images they associate with retiring that matters. Now you might think that talking about retirement is harmless, but remember, the subconscious also works by means of association. What kind of things do you associate with retirement? Are they positive or negative? If the image you have of retirement is one of being poverty stricken, unattractive, and in poor health, then this is what your subconscious takes as a "goal" and sets out to achieve. Some people reinforce it further by allowing retirement to control their actions. They say things like, "Now that I've retired, I'm entitled to a free bus pass." Now don't get me wrong, I'm not saying these people don't deserve free bus passes or anything like that. What I am saying is that the subconscious doesn't usually associate free bus passes and retirement with wealth or being young. It usually associates it with poverty, poor health, disability, and the like. Some people even start to give themselves negative titles, such as "old age pensioner," but if that's what you want, then go ahead and say it, but if that's not what you want, then why say it? All of these things contribute to the overall picture you have of yourself. The more things, the more definite the picture and the higher the chance of making it a reality.

It is virtually impossible to stay young-looking if you're providing the subconscious with such negative goals or images. On the positive side, the people I know who have reached their later years and still look young also act young. They refuse to let "age" be a determining factor in their lives. They don't speak about being old and they certainly don't refer to themselves as an "old age pensioner." Instead, they live very busy and active lives. Many of them still keep fit, still go on holidays abroad, and still socialise with their friends. Some of them still do some form of work, and they couldn't care less about free bus passes, because they still drive. Therefore, the picture they have of themselves is still one of a young person. Why change it?

"To retire is to expire."
(Unknown)

Here are some examples of affirmations that you might find helpful. Most people prefer to make their own, because everyone's situation is unique. Remember, to make an affirmation, you first need to identify the problem (this means being brutally honest with yourself), then affirm what you want. (Which is the opposite.)

PROBLEM (NEVER say this):	SAY THIS INSTEAD:
I hate speaking in public.	I love public speaking.
I'm terrible at public speaking.	I am a great public speaker.
I feel self conscious and inferior compared to other people.	I am confident in everything I do. I'm as good as anyone else.
I don't feel worthy of success.	God created me to succeed. I deserve success.
I have failed at most things in my life.	I succeed in everything I do. God is on my side.
There are things about myself that I don't like.	I love who I am. I'm happy with myself.
I don't think I'm a very interesting speaker.	I am so enthusiastic! People love hearing me talk.
I don't feel too good today.	I feel great!
I feel slightly weak.	I have unlimited strength.
I'm not very good at a certain sport.	Every day I'm getting better and better at—.
I can't be bothered.	I'm fired up and full of energy.
I never seem to get ahead.	I am a winner; I always find a way to succeed.
Things never seem to be straightforward.	Things are simple if you tell yourself they're simple.
People seldom talk to me.	I meet lots of interesting people every day. People are attracted to me.
This seems like a big problem.	This seems like a big opportunity.

FINANCIAL:
- I am now making £____ a year (state specific amount).
- I'm getting richer every day.
- I live a life of abundance, increasing wealth and prosperity.
- I am rich, and I deserve to be rich.

SPIRITUAL:
- God created me for success.
- God has no favorites, I'm as important as anyone else.
- God is with me every second of every day.
- I can do all things through Christ who strengthens me.

PROFANITY

Another thing that will adversely affect your state of mind is profanity, or the use of swear words. When your state of mind is negative, you attract negative things and negative people. As mentioned earlier, when you speak words, you don't just program your mind with words, you program it with emotion. The emotion behind the words is what will affect your subconscious the most. Most people who use swear words usually do so with negative emotions such as anger, frustration, hatred, and the like, although there are many other negative emotions that lie behind swear words.

When you program yourself with negative emotions, you are programming yourself to fail. You cannot be happy and experience negative emotions at the same time, because happiness is a positive emotion. You might curse and swear and think you are releasing negative emotions, but this is an illusion. Instead, when you curse and swear you are actually "creating" negative emotions, and you feel even worse afterwards. For example, if something or someone caused you to experience anger, you might think you are releasing anger by swearing, but you will end up even more angry, because anger is the emotion behind the words. If you don't believe me, think about how you feel after an argument. Do you feel happier, or less happy? The reason you don't feel very happy afterwards is because the words you have spoken were backed up with negative emotions, and this is what impacts your subconscious mind the most.

Think about it. If you feel less happy after an argument than you did before it, what made the difference? The answer is words. Words, backed up with emotion, changed your state of mind. That is the power of words! I'm not saying it's wrong to get involved in an argument; what I'm saying is that if we believe we are absolutely right, then we can still state our case without using swear words, and, as a result, our emotions will still be positive. Now that is an example of using words negatively. So if negative words adversely affect our state of mind, then it stands to reason that the opposite must hold true; that positive words backed with positive emotion must improve our state of mind and make us feel happier. For example, think about how good you feel when you give someone a sincere compliment. Yes, it makes them feel good, but it also makes you feel good too, because of the positive emotions created by it. It's a win-win situation. Think about how you feel when you say to someone, "I love you." Your state of mind, as well as theirs, was greatly enhanced, simply because of three little words. They may only be three little words, but they have a lot of emotion behind them.

One of the worst things about swear words is that they cut us off from God. When we swear, it offends the Holy Spirit who dwells within us, and spiritually we feel distant from God. The same can be said of negative emotions. It is impossible to feel close to God and also experience peace while you are suffering from negative emotions. I don't know about you, but I don't like feeling distant from God. Swear words are like a barrier you create between yourself and God, and you will be less happy.

If you don't believe swear words affect your state of

mind, the problem could be that you have become so used to it that you don't notice it and are unaware that you have created a negative state of mind. If so, why not try the thirty-day test? For thirty days, use no swear words or any kind of profanity. The reason for the thirty-day test is to give you a mental comparison between the two different states of mind. If you slip up and use a swear word, your thirty days begins all over again (even if you were on day twenty-nine). Do this until you have completed your thirty days. At the end of the thirty days check your attitude and your emotions and compare them to what they were before. (By the way, if you don't normally swear, then there is no need to take the test). Give yourself a pat on the back. You probably already have a good vocabulary. But if this does apply to you, then don't you feel much better? Hasn't your attitude toward other people changed? Hasn't your attitude in general changed? Don't you feel happier? If we use swear words (or disobey God in general), we also reduce the chances of our prayers being answered. The Bible tells us, "The prayer of a righteous man is powerful and effective." (James 5:16)." We cannot be swearing like a trooper and still expect God to answer us favourably.

for X-FACTOR

You might be thinking, what is the X-factor? The X-factor can be whatever you want. The X-factor is something that can make the difference between success and failure, or happiness and unhappiness. The reason I have called it the X-factor is because it is chosen. Some people choose to have it, some people don't. In this case I have chosen to make the X-factor the spiritual side of our lives. If you don't believe in God then you might want to skip this chapter and go on to chapter "Y." As a Christian, I can only speak from my own point of view, but I sincerely hope that you do not skip this chapter, but instead, read it with an open mind.

I often hear people saying, "How do you know the Bible is true, and not just some made up fairytale?" Well most people who I've heard saying that have never read the Bible. I don't mean necessarily the whole Bible, but usually they have read either very little or nothing at all. So how can they have an opinion on something they know nothing about? If this applies to you, why not read it first and then see if you feel the same way? I challenge anyone to read the Bible and not be convinced it is the true word of God. Firstly, I don't think men could be that wise. Take, for example, the words of wisdom found in the book of Proverbs, and try putting some of these principles into practice and see if they come true. Man hasn't got the power to make principles like that come true, let alone create them! So why do they come true if there is not a God? Who created the principles? Some people even think that parts of the Bible no longer apply. Some people pick and choose the bits they like and disbelieve the rest. For example, some people believe in God, but don't believe there is a Hell. Some people think the Old Testament no longer applies. If this was the case, it would mean that parts of the Bible aren't true, which would make God a liar, which would make Him a sinner. And that's never going to happen. The Bible says, "All Scripture is God-breathed and is useful for teaching, correcting, and training in righteousness, so that the man of God may be thoroughly equipped for every good work." (2 Tim 3:16-17)

The Bible doesn't have a sell-by date or expiry date on it, and never will. We must remember that God is not only a loving God, he is also a "just" God. This means that He has to be fair. He has to punish sin as well as reward the righteous. If God were to let evil people of the hook, it wouldn't be fair. And if the righteous were to go unrewarded, it wouldn't be fair either. But thankfully He is a just God, as well as a loving and forgiving God. If anyone doubts this, they only need to look up Leviticus 26 and Deuteronomy 28. There are things I have read in the Bible that, if I had known them years ago, I'm certain I would have avoided a lot of the pitfalls I fell into. The Bible is wisdom. It is the Handbook for success and happiness and has been referred to as Basic Instructions Before Leaving Earth. (BIBLE).

Secondly, why do we reap what we sow? Why does that principle hold true if there isn't a God? Who created the principle? Even unbelievers recognise this principle. A principle cannot create itself. Some far greater Force has to have created it. Man cannot create it. The Bible says, "A generous man will prosper." (Prov 11:25) Why is it that when we give money away, we get even more in return? Try it and see. Yet logic would tell us that if we give, we will end up with less. But this is a lie, and also the work of the devil.

Remember that faith has no logic. Sometimes faith requires us to go against logic. When the apostle Peter got out of the boat and walked on water, logic says he should have sunk, but he didn't. Logic doesn't come into it when you have faith. It's not our job to figure out "how," but only to believe. Never get bogged down trying to figure out "how." Forget about "how" and have faith instead. "How" is none of our business!

I remember a woman telling me about a time when she and her husband were walking along the street and there was a homeless person sitting on the pavement begging for money. She only had a few pounds left, but she gave it to them anyway. It was a very small amount, but it was also her last. Her husband suddenly said, "Why did you do that? It's all we had left!" Anyway, when they got home, there was an unexpected cheque lying there for a much greater amount. Obviously, where the cheque had come from had nothing to do with the homeless person— or did it?

While I admit that nothing can be proven, the point I want to make and the thing I want you to consider is why do these principles hold true? To an unbeliever it would seem like coincidence, but that's exactly how God works! God isn't going to suddenly jump down and appear before us and say, "That was me who did that!" He doesn't need to because He has already written it in the Bible to forewarn us. He wants us to have faith in His word. Anyone can believe in what is seen, but it takes a person of faith to believe in the unseen. Many times it does seem like coincidence, but it isn't our job to figure that out. The Bible simply says that if you do certain things, there will be certain results (this goes for good and evil). Certain actions will bring rewards and certain actions will bring consequences. It doesn't say "how" it will happen; it just says that it "will" happen. Neither does God put a timeframe on it.

Often we read or hear about Gods principles, and if it doesn't happen when we think it should, we tend to doubt it.

But this is because we ourselves put a timeframe on it, and we shouldn't. I must admit there have been times when I have been guilty of doing this, and I shouldn't. Sometimes results happen quickly; other times they take much longer, but they will happen.

Another question we often hear is, "Why does God allow the innocent to suffer?" I don't know, and I don't believe anyone knows, at least not in this lifetime. But I do believe that God tests our faith, and I also believe that one day we will understand. Some people say, "Where was God when this happened?" or "Where was God when that happened?" He was in exactly the same place as He was when his Son was dying on the cross. So if He allowed His own Son to die for our sins, to take the punishment that we deserve, then it helps to put things into perspective. Also, remember that God often uses adversity to teach us, correct us, and discipline us. He has to get our attention, otherwise we might continue in our foolish ways, on a path to destruction. When God does this, He doesn't do it because He likes to see us suffer; He does it because He loves us and wants to save us. Often adversity can turn out to be a blessing in disguise and the beginning of a new opportunity.

On the subject of allowing the innocent to suffer, consider what happened to Job in the Old Testament. Job was a very honest man and was also very wealthy. He owned seven thousand sheep, three thousand camels, five hundred yoke of oxen and five hundred donkeys, and had a large number of servants. He was very faithful to God, and was blameless in the sight of the Lord. The Lord said to Satan, "Have you considered my servant Job? There is no one on earth like him; he is blameless and upright, a man who fears God and shuns evil."

"Does Job fear God for nothing," Satan replied. "Have you not put a hedge around him and his household and everything he has? You have blessed the work of his hands, so that his flocks and herds are spread throughout the land.

But stretch out your hand and strike everything he has and he will surely curse you to your face."

The Lord said to Satan, "Very well, then, everything he has is in your hands, but on the man himself do not lay a finger." Then Satan went out from the presence of the Lord.

One day when Jobs sons and daughters were feasting and drinking wine at the oldest brother's house, a messenger came to Job and said, "The oxen were ploughing and the donkeys were grazing nearby, and the Sabeans attacked and carried them off. They put the servants to the sword and I am the only one who has escaped to tell you!"

While he was still speaking, another messenger came and said, "The fire of God fell from the sky and burned up the sheep and the servants, and I am the only one who has escaped to tell you!"

While he was still speaking, another messenger came and said, "The Chaldeans formed three raiding parties and swept down on your camels and carried them off. They put the servants to the sword, and I am the only one who has escaped to tell you!"

While he was still speaking, yet another messenger came and said, "Your sons and daughters were feasting and drinking wine at the oldest brothers house, when suddenly a mighty wind swept in from the desert and struck the four corners of the house. It collapsed on them and they are dead, and I am the only one who has escaped to tell you!" (Job 1:8-19) But, "In all this, Job did not sin by charging God with wrongdoing." (v. 22) Job could easily have cursed God because he had done nothing wrong. Instead, he said, "Naked I came from my mother's womb, and naked I shall depart. The Lord gave and the Lord has taken away; may the name of the Lord be praised." (v. 21)

The devil went on to tempt God further by saying that if God would allow Job's health to suffer, surely he would curse God then. Satan said to the Lord, "A man will give all he has for his own life. But stretch out your hand and strike his flesh and bones and he will surely curse you to your face."

The Lord said to Satan, "Very well, then, he is in your hands; but you must spare his life." So Satan went out from the presence of the Lord and afflicted Job with painful sores from the soles of his feet to the top of his head. (Job 2:7) "In all this, Job did not sin in what he said." (Job 2:10) Job's suffering was so great that he began to curse the day he was born. Yet despite all of this, he remained faithful to God.

But at the end of the book of Job, we are told, "The Lord made him prosperous again and gave him twice as much as he had before." (Job 42:10) The Lord blessed the latter part of Job's life more than the first. He had fourteen thousand sheep, six thousand camels, a thousand yoke of oxen, and a thousand donkeys." (Job 42:12). After this, Job lived a hundred and forty years; he saw his children and their children to the fourth generation. And so he died, old and full of years." (Job 42:16).

So why did God allow Job to suffer when he was blameless and innocent? Because God had to prove his point to the devil. God had to prove the devil wrong. Why do I tell that story? Because we don't know the reasons behind our suffering. Could it be that the same dialogue is taking place between God and Satan in our own lives? Who knows! The reasons are beyond our comprehension. That's why we need to have faith. Because we don't know what's going on behind the scenes. God knows exactly what's going on.

I think David Pawson explains this point very well. He likened the suffering on earth to the suffering during the Vietnam War. He said that the root cause of the suffering in the local Vietnamese villages was not caused by local conflict, but was the result of a far greater war that was going on, namely the war between North and South. The root cause of the suffering in the local villages was actually a symptom of a war between Capitalism and Communism. And only when the war between North and South was settled, would there be peace in the local villages.

In the same way, the root cause of all the suffering in the world today is not caused by itself, but is a symptom of a far greater war which is going on, namely the war between God and Satan. And only when Satan is finally thrown into the abyss, will there be no more evil. One day the devil and his angels will be eternally separated from God and his people. Some people think that the devil is in hell. He is not; he is in the world. That's why there's so much evil in the world. Remember that the devil was at one time an angel in heaven, but because of his pride and saying that he would make himself like the Most High, he was thrown out. The Bible says, "And there was war in heaven. Michael and his angels fought against the dragon and the dragon and his angels fought back. But he was not strong enough and they lost their place in heaven. The great dragon was hurled down— that ancient serpent called the devil, or Satan, who leads the whole world astray. He was hurled to earth and his angels with him." (Rev 12:7-9) Two-thirds of the angels stayed loyal to God, but a third followed the devil to earth. These are now known as demons, or evil spirits.

The book of Job also backs this up. In the first two chapters we see the angels presenting themselves before the Lord, and Satan going along with them. And the Lord said to Satan, "Where have you come from?" Satan answered the Lord, "From roaming through the earth and going to and fro in it." (Job 1:7, 2:2)

Some people are unaware that our lives are a constant daily struggle between two forces; the forces of good and the forces of evil. On one hand, God is calling us to obedience because He wants us to live a life of abundance, happiness, and prosperity. On the other hand, Satan is opposed to everything God stands for and is in favour of everything God is against. He does this by lying, tempting, tricking, and deceiving, and unfortunately he is very clever at doing so. The devil's ways are vast and varied, probably too numerous to mention. Another way Satan accomplishes his work is by working through people. We can clearly see this in the world of politics. Just as God works through people for good purposes, Satan does the same thing for evil purposes.

The Bible says, "Watch out for false prophets. They come to you in sheep's clothing, but inwardly they are ferocious wolves." (Mat 7:15). The Bible tells us that Satan often accomplishes evil in such a way that it often appears to look good. "For such men are false prophets, deceitful workmen masquerading as apostles of Christ. And no wonder, for Satan himself masquerades as an angel of light. It is not surprising then if his servants masquerade as servants of righteousness. (2 Cor 11:13-15).

Could this have anything to do with the deceptive titles of "equality" or "human rights?" While there is nothing wrong with equality or human rights, there is something wrong when "human rights" is used as an excuse for protecting wrongdoers. Don't be deceived! There is never an excuse for sin in God's eyes.

The best way to find out if something is deceptive or not is to see how it compares to the word of God. If it conflicts with the Bible, then it is the work of the devil. The problem with deception is that people who have been deceived don't believe they have been deceived. Even if you were to point it out to them and it was blatantly obvious, they would still refuse to believe. That's because they've been deceived! That's how the devil wins his battles on earth!

But on a positive note, Satan's time is short and it is limited. One day we will be eternally free from his influence and power. The power Satan has on earth at the moment is also limited by God. There is nothing Satan can do without God allowing it. We are told that "He whose walk is blameless is kept safe." (Prov 28:18)

Another thing we often hear people saying is, "You can't take it with you!" Usually they're referring to money or material possessions when they say this. And they're absolutely right! In this life we actually own nothing. God owns everything! We are simply stewards over what He has entrusted us with and He will judge us accordingly. We came into this world with nothing and we will depart with nothing— except for one thing. There is one thing we will take with us, and that is our deeds. The Bible tells us, "Nothing in all creation is hidden from God's sight. Everything is uncovered and laid bare before the eyes of him to whom we must give account." (Heb 4:13)

Some day Christ is going to return. The day and hour are unknown. But this time He will come back in glory to judge the living and the dead. One thing is for sure, and that is there will be no mistaking it when it happens, because He will appear in the sky, visible to everyone.

"For as lightning that comes from the east is visible even in the west, so will be the coming of the Son of Man." (Mat 24:27) The Bible tells us that it will happen at a time when we least expect it, like a thief in the night. "At that time the sign of the Son of Man will appear in the sky, and all the nations of the earth will mourn. They will see the Son of Man coming on the clouds of the sky with power and great glory. And he will send his angels with a loud trumpet call, and they will gather his elect from the four winds, from one end of the heavens to the other." (Mat 24:30-31).

"Two men will be in the field; one will be taken and the other left. Two women will be grinding with a hand mill; one will be taken and the other left. Therefore, keep watch, because you do not know on what day your Lord will come." (Mat 24:40-42).

So why does God tell us all this? Is it to frighten us? He does it because He wants to save us. Never forget that the God who wrote these words is the same God who died on the cross for us. I just want you to pause for a moment and try to comprehend eternity. Many of us probably don't think about it because we often get so wrapped up in our daily lives that day-to-day living becomes our only focus. I personally find eternity hard to comprehend. It boggles the mind. When will it end? NEVER! Yet each one of us will spend it some place.

Imagine, for a moment, a sandy beach. Now try and see how many grains of sand there are on that beach. Quite a few! Now imagine all the beaches of the world combined. How many grains of sand would that be? Now imagine that each grain of sand represented a million years. How many years would that equal? Blows the mind, doesn't it? Well, understand that if you added all of them up, eternity would have hardly even begun. Yet every one of us will spend eternity somewhere. Even if you lived until you were 120, how does that compare to eternity? It doesn't, does it?

Of course, God still wants us to live our lives to the full. Of course He wants us to be successful. Of course He wants us to be prosperous and be happy, but it all must be within the realms of obedience. God doesn't want us to become so preoccupied with earthly things that we lose sight of Heavenly things. The Bible says, "Blessed are those who wash their robes, that they may have the right to the tree of life and may go through the gates into the city. Outside are the dogs, those who practice magic arts, the sexually immoral, the murderers, the idolaters and everyone who loves and practices falsehood." (Rev 22:14-15).

But bear in mind that it's never too late to repent and ask for God's forgiveness. It doesn't matter what you've done up until now; if you repent and change your ways, God will forgive you. "If we confess our sins, he is faithful and just and will forgive us our sins and purify us from all unrighteousness." (1 John 1: 9)

"He is patient with you, not wanting anyone to perish, but everyone to come to repentance." (2 Pet 3:9)

The Bible says God is going to create a new heaven and new earth. Can you imagine a place where only righteousness dwells? A place where we are reunited with loved ones, forever! Where there is no more illness or sickness or pain? Where there is no need for hospitals? Where there is no more unhappiness, but only love and joy? Imagine no more hatred or wars. No more killing or terrorism. No more violence. No more stealing or selfishness. No more greed, jealousy, or fear. No more political sleaze or lies. No more crime. No need for a police force or army because there is no evil. No more cruel dictators or tyrants. No more anger, bitterness, or rage. No more ill feeling. A place where only love exists!

But before God creates the new, He must get rid of the old. He must clear away everything which is unholy and impure. Jesus said, "'In my Father's house are many rooms; if it were not so, I would have told you. I am going there to prepare a place for you. And if I go and prepare a place for you, I will come back and take you to be with me that you also may be where I am. You know the way to the place where I am going.' Thomas said to him, 'Lord, we don't know where you are going, so how can we know the way?' Jesus answered, 'I am the way and the truth and the life. No one comes to the Father except through me. If you really knew me, you would know my Father as well. From now on, you do know him and have seen him.'" (John 14:1-7).

> "No eye has seen,
> no ear has heard,
> no mind has conceived
> what God has prepared for those
> who love him."
> (1 Cor 2:9)

for YESTERDAY

Are you living for today, or are you letting the past drag you down? Are you focusing on your dreams and what your future holds, or are you dwelling on the mistakes of the past? Maybe you're still clinging to yesterday's successes and talking about the "good old days?" Either way, it's going to hold you back in the present. Yesterday is gone forever. Today is a new day and the chance to begin again. Today is an opportunity to focus on your dreams and what lies ahead rather than to live in the past.

A camera cannot clearly focus on something far away and something up close at the same time. It has to be one or the other. If it focuses on something up close, everything else will be vague. If it focuses on something far away, then the things that are up close will be cloudy and vague. Focusing on one thing will always be at the exclusion of the other. Our minds work in the same way. We cannot clearly focus on what happened yesterday and our dreams at the same time. It has to be one or the other.

Of course we sometimes need to refer to the past, in order to learn from it or analyse it, but we shouldn't dwell on it or live there mentally. Once the lesson is learned, it should be forgotten. Someone once said that the past is a good guide but it is a bad hitching post. For some of us the past has been relatively positive, but for others it may be something we would rather forget. I don't believe anyone's past has been totally positive and I don't believe anyone's past has been totally negative. Even someone with a relatively positive past has experienced some hardship and pain, and someone with a mainly negative past has experienced the occasional "happy moment."

The purpose of this chapter is to get you to focus on the right things so that you can move forward toward your dreams. If your past hasn't been positive, stop dwelling on it and stop digging it up. If you've made mistakes in the past, make sure that you learn from them and try not to repeat them. Our focus should be similar to that when we're driving a car. What would happen if instead of looking at the road in front of us we were constantly looking at the rear view mirror? We would probably crash! When we're driving, we need to keep our eyes constantly focused on where we're going if we want to successfully get to our destination. The rearview mirror should only be glanced at from time to time; so it should be with our past. Remember that whatever you focus on becomes the "goal" for your subconscious to achieve. Therefore, if you're focusing too much on mistakes of the past, the mistakes themselves become the goal for your subconscious, and you're likely to repeat them. Instead, we need to be focusing on our dreams.

Some people get so concerned about the progress of other people that they start comparing themselves to them. If other people are way ahead of them, they get depressed, and if other people haven't achieved as much, they feel good. But this is pointless, because you are not in competition with anyone but yourself. Forget about what other people are doing. Their success does not determine your success and their failure has no bearing on whether you will fail or not. Being overly concerned about the achievements of others is almost as bad as dwelling on the past. It's similar to driving a car, but you're neither looking ahead nor looking at the rear view mirror. Instead, you're constantly looking out the side window at all the passing shops and buildings. Do you think you would safely get to your destination? Probably not! So why do it? It doesn't matter what someone else achieved yesterday and it doesn't matter what you've failed to achieve. Today is a new beginning.

Sometimes people ask me, "What did you have for your dinner yesterday?" and I have to admit, I often can't remember. It's not that there's anything wrong with my memory, but it simply isn't important enough for me to try and remember. I'm more concerned about what I'm having for dinner later on tonight because it's in the future. My focus is constantly forward. Remember that focusing on one thing is always at the exclusion of the other.

YOU CAN'T CHANGE THE PAST, SO DON'T TRY TO

Some people beat themselves up and rip themselves to shreds because of the mistakes they made yesterday. They say things to themselves like, "You fool!" "You idiot!" "How could you be so dumb?" But this is pointless, because no matter how much you regret what happened yesterday or how angry you are at yourself, all these negative words are not going to change a thing. So why do it? Remember that such negative words are also affirmations and will create an even more negative state of mind. Do you want to be a fool? Do you want to do foolish things and fail some more? Then why call yourself such things? Why program yourself to act that way? Because that's exactly what you're doing. No amount of regret, anger, or worrying will change what happened a few seconds ago, let alone yesterday. Some people say, "If only I had done this" or "I wish I hadn't done that." Although we may regret what we did or didn't do, the only thing we can do is learn from it. Sometimes that's all we can salvage from it. If you have messed up really badly, there is nothing that God can't help you to put right again. No problem is too big for God. Why not ask for His help?

You may have messed up because of an unwise decision, or it could be because your actions were based on negative emotions, such as greed, anger, fear, or even hatred. Although we can't change the past, we can change what we do from this moment onward. If you have hurt someone or offended them, you can't change the fact that you did that, but you can change how you treat them from this moment onward. That is within your control and always will be. You can, if you wish, commit to a different course of behaviour from now on.

If you are to become successful, you need to view your mistakes and regrets as part of the learning curve, because they are. God wants you to overcome your past, not get bogged down by it. When you mess up, the main thing is to look for the lesson to be learned and then change your behavior accordingly. Remember that failure is part of success. If you want great success, you've got to be willing to endure great failure. Being bitter toward ourselves because of what we did yesterday will only add fuel to the fire of negative emotions. It will also cause us to lose focus and lose sight of our dreams.

Secondly, realise that you are only human, and we all mess up from time to time. Instead of hating yourself or being angry at yourself, use that energy to focus on how you would handle that situation differently if it were to occur again. Examine your mistake and see where you went wrong. Once you have identified it, try to figure out how you should have handled it. If a similar situation arises in the future, put your new strategy into practice. Often this is the complete opposite of how we did handle it. Then, instead of getting mad at yourself, forgive yourself and move on. Realise that this has actually contributed to your personal development, not detracted from it. By viewing mistakes in this way, you'll be growing from them and learning from them. This is what many successful people call "failing your way to success."

But it is not always the mistakes of yesterday that can bog us down. The mistakes we made a few seconds ago can also trouble us unless we get our attitude right. But they will only trouble us if we allow them to. We have to give our permission first. I remember hearing an American football player talking about how his team's thinking toward their mistakes played a huge part in whether they won or lost. Every time he made a mistake on the field, not only did he have thousands of fans shouting abuse at him, he also had to immediately flush the mistake out of his mind or it would mess him up for the next move. It was impossible to be thinking about his mistake and be thinking about the next move at the same time. Often, he would only have seconds to do this. So he had to get mentally tough and train himself to be constantly thinking about the next move, no matter what mistake he had just made. He couldn't afford to live mentally in the past, not even for a split second.

The past will only affect your future if you let it. You may have had an experience in the past where you attempted to do something outside your comfort zone, such as speak in public for the first time, and you messed up really badly. Don't worry if you did, you're not alone! The main thing is how you face it the next time (future). If you regard yourself as a failure (negative self talk) and talk about failure, (how you failed last time), you will go into your next experience with a picture of failure, and you will attract failure. You will literally drag the past into the future and recreate it unless you focus on a picture of success. Your subconscious will take it as a goal and help to bring it about. Instead, you need to smash that negative picture of failure and replace it with a picture of success. How do you do that? You do it with words. Remember what we said in an earlier chapter? That words are more powerful than mental images? Therefore words of success will override the negative mental image of failure that you have and replace it with an image of success. Instead of dwelling on or talking about past failures, tell yourself that you are an excellent public speaker. Tell yourself that you are confident and enthusiastic. Don't let a word of failure be heard on your lips. And don't mention a word of past failures either. Don't focus on it and don't think about it. It doesn't matter anymore; it's gone forever. Tell yourself this is a new day, a new beginning, and you are an excellent speaker NOW. Then you'll approach your next talk with more confidence and a better chance of performing well.

If you look at the lives of extremely successful people, you'll find that they also endured great failure. Abraham Lincoln and Thomas Edison immediately come to mind, along with many others.   But they didn't allow the mistakes of yesterday to shape their tomorrows. Instead, they viewed their mistakes as part of the learning curve toward success and took the attitude that every day is a new beginning and the chance to begin again.

LEARN FROM YOUR SUCCESSES
AS WELL AS YOUR FAILURES

If you are wise, you will let the mistakes of yesterday become a guide for tomorrow. You will learn what worked and what didn't work. You will learn what to repeat and what not to repeat. Yesterday can be an excellent teacher if we will only learn its lessons. We only become foolish if we fail to learn from it. Only a fool would repeat behaviour which was detrimental to their success. But at the same time, we should also be wise enough to learn from our successes. If something works, then keep doing it! And if it didn't work, stop doing it!

Someone once said that the height of insanity is to keep doing the same thing over and over, expecting different results. A bit like the hamster in the wheel saying to itself, "If I just keep doing what I'm doing, I'm sure the scenery will eventually get better."

Sorry to disappoint you, hamster!

But some people's lives are like that. They're maybe repeating negative habits that they've had for most of their lives and wondering why they don't have a better lifestyle. They want better results, but they don't want to change their habits. They say things like, "It's just the way I am." But it's not the way they are, it's the way they "think" they are. There's a big difference. If you say "It's just the way I am," you're giving away your power to your past and allowing it to control you. Don't let that happen! Instead, take responsibility and decide to change.

How are your results at the moment? Not just financially, but also in terms of relationships, health, and happiness. Are you where you want to be in life? Have you met your ideal partner? Are you doing what you want to do on a daily basis? Realise that what you did yesterday helped to create where you are today.

If you're not satisfied with a particular area in your life, could it be that you're repeating the same old mistakes and have failed to learn the lesson? Could it be that sexual immorality is keeping you from meeting the ideal partner? Could it be that a lack of exercise or too much junk food is keeping you from having a healthy body? Could it be that watching the news and reading newspapers is depressing you and keeping you from happiness?

Could it be that poor financial habits are keeping you broke? Could it be that a drug or alcohol addiction is keeping you from becoming successful and is stealing your dreams? Could it be that negative words are causing you to have a negative emotional state? If you aren't satisfied in a particular area, check your behaviour and your habits. Is it time to make a change?

You might be saying to yourself, "But I've always done these things." Well, have you ever thought to yourself, "Maybe I've always done these things, but maybe that's also the problem?" Maybe it's because I've always done these things, that I've always had the same results? Maybe I'm allowing my past to control my future? Just because that's your past doesn't mean it has to be your future. You can decide at any point to change what you do in the present.

When you change what you do in the present, you will create a different future. For your lifestyle to change, your habits have to change first.

YOUR PAST DOES NOT DETERMINE YOUR FUTURE

You might not have any of these problems, and if not, I congratulate you! You're obviously doing something right. Keep doing it! But if we're not careful, the past can also have devastating psychological effects on us. I remember the story of one woman who had an extremely negative past in terms of relationships. Her past had affected her so much that she had a poor self image. She had suffered abuse and it had affected her beliefs. She thought of herself as ugly, even though she was very attractive. She thought she was fat, even though she had a lovely figure. In fact, she had virtually no fat on her. The problem was that her beliefs had been messed up because of years of abuse. She had been subjected to put-downs and negative comments so often and for such a long period of time that her subconscious had accepted it as "fact" even though it was a lie. The other problem was that she couldn't see her future as being any different from her past. And that is a very dangerous mode of thinking to get into, because what we believe will become our reality.

Sadly, many people, through ignorance of how the mind works, allow a negative past to become their future. But it doesn't have to be. That's the saddest part! Some people believe we are born into certain slots in life and there's no escape. They think that some people were meant to succeed and others were meant to fail. They think that you're stuck where you are. This is another great lie, because what we ultimately become in life is chosen. Perhaps I should say "who" we become is chosen, because it is. Every day we are choosing who we become by how we think, by the words we speak, by our emotional responses, by our actions, and by what we allow into our minds.

This woman was in the habit of using negative words and saying what she "didn't" want, such as, "Men, they're all the same!" or "I always seem to attract the wrong guys," until someone pointed out to her that unless she changed her words, she would keep getting more of the same. They helped her to understand that what you say is what you get, and your words become a self-fulfilling prophecy. They told her that, regardless of what had happened in the past, there was no reason her future had to be the same. But she had to make some changes. It all started with her, and she alone was responsible for her future. The reason she was attracting those types of guys was because she had unknowingly programmed her subconscious mind to attract them. She even began to feel as though she "deserved" the abuse, which added fuel to the fire. The truth is that no one deserves abuse!

She was also in the habit of "being too good to them," to the point that they would walk all over her, in a proverbial sense. They helped her to see that, because her behaviour hadn't changed, her results hadn't changed either, and neither would they until she changed first. So she began to change the words she spoke. She began saying daily affirmations, such as:

> "Everyone I meet is friendly, honest and sincere."
>
> "I am very happy and have met the man of my dreams."
>
> "He treats me with respect because I am a respectable person."
>
> "I deserve to meet nice people because I am a nice person."
>
> "People tell me I'm beautiful and have a lovely figure."
>
> "I am confident, strong, and attractive."

In other words, she decided to put her foot down and that the past was no longer going to have a hold on her. She also decided that she was going to play harder to get and take a slightly tougher line with potential partners. No longer would she be a "walkover." She would start laying down some rules, and if they didn't like it, TOUGH! She would find somebody else. She also began reading positive books instead of fashion magazines, and as a result, her self image improved. It dawned on her that as long as she was comparing herself to models in these magazines, she was bound to feel bad. She began to realise the truth about herself instead of believing the lies she had always believed. By changing what went into her mind, she also began to develop self confidence. She no longer felt unattractive, but she began to realise that she was a creation of God, and that many people indeed found her attractive. And because she changed the way she saw herself, other people began to see her differently, too. She became fun to be around and was very popular and well liked, but it all began with a change in thinking.

Change always takes place mentally before you see any outward improvements. We all need to break free from the chains of the past! The past has no bearing on your potential. You've always had the potential, you just don't believe it. Even when you were going through your darkest days, you still had the potential deep down inside of you. Stop giving yourself negative labels or you will NEVER realise your potential. If you have messed up badly in the past, forgive yourself and move on!

If you have faced a situation in the past which involved facing your fears and you performed badly, one of two things probably happened: either you felt so bad that you never tried it again and labelled yourself as a failure in that area (negative self talk), or you persisted and eventually overcame your fear. Sadly, many people choose the former. When I first spoke in public, I felt so bad that I wished the ground had opened up beneath me and swallowed me in. No joke! But I knew that if I didn't try it again, the fear would control my life. So I thought, "I don't care how badly I perform next time, nothing is as bad as having fear control my life." I was not going to allow my past to control my future. I also had faith that through persistence I would eventually improve, and I did— just as you will!

If I had decided not to speak in public again, not only would I have closed off the opportunity to become better, but I would have continued to hold a false belief about myself that I was a terrible public speaker. This lie would then have controlled my life. We need to realise that we are not failures because we have failed, but we are people with great potential who sometimes fail on the road to success. There is nothing in your past that needs to have any control over your future unless you let it.

Some people might feel that because they've done things in the past that they're ashamed of, they can never move on and become successful in the future. This is another lie.

I've got news for you, you're not alone! You've got company! I don't think there's a human being walking the planet who doesn't have regrets about the past. Of course, some things are more serious than others, but it makes no difference to God if you have truly repented and changed your ways. There was only one Person who walked on this earth who had no regrets about the past, and they crucified Him. So realise that making mistakes and doing things you regret is part of being human. But it is equally important that we don't use this as a cop-out or excuse for doing wrong. If we know something is wrong, we need stop immediately and get ourselves right with God.

I remember hearing a prison chaplain speaking about his visit to a prison to speak with some of the prisoners. One of them was doing a life sentence for murder. He had been in jail for many years and was truly sorry for his crime. He had confessed his sins to God and had asked for His forgiveness. He deeply regretted what he had done and had begun studying the Bible. He had also developed the habit of re-programming his mind with positive material, but he found it hard to believe that God could forgive him for such a hideous crime, let alone society.

The chaplain pointed out to him that mentally and physically he was no longer the same person as the person who committed the crime. Obviously his DNA was still the same, but mentally he was no longer the same person because of the change in his thoughts, emotions, attitude, and most importantly, his heart. Physically he was also a different person too, because our subconscious mind is constantly renewing every cell in our body. Therefore, mentally and physically he was a different person.

Now don't get me wrong here, I'm not saying that people should get out early or anything like it. I think the punishment should fit the crime and people should see it through to the end. But what I am saying and what the chaplain was referring to is God's forgiveness. We may still have to face the consequences of our sin here on earth, but if we have truly repented, God isn't going to hold it against us on the Day of Judgment.

When a person truly repents and turns to Christ, ALL is forgiven. No exceptions. The Bible says, "Therefore, if anyone is in Christ, he is a new creation; the old has gone, the new has come! All this is from God who reconciled us to himself through Christ and gave us the ministry of reconciliation: that God was reconciling the world to himself in Christ, not counting men's sins against them." (2 Cor 5:17-19). When Jesus died on the cross, He took the punishment for the sins of the world.

While that might be an extreme example, the principle is the same for all of us. We needn't allow the mistakes of the past to become a burden for tomorrow. Every day is a gift from God, and our focus should always be on where we are going, not on where we have been.

for ZEAL

The dictionary defines the word 'zeal' as meaning 'great enthusiasm' or 'eagerness'. And that is exactly what we need if we are to achieve our dreams in life. When we have great enthusiasm or eagerness, it increases our energy and we can go further than we normally could have had we lacked this positive energy.

When you're fired up about achieving something, you often find that you don't need as much sleep because of the increased energy that you have. You look forward to getting up, instead of dreading it, because you have something in life to aim for. You have something that excites you. You might even feel that sleep is getting in the way because you have so much to do and so much to accomplish, but you don't care because you're fired up! You are excited about your future!

Zeal is a very positive emotion that creates energy in your physical body, strengthens your immune system, and makes you less likely to catch disease. This energy radiates from you, and people can tell that you're fired up. If other people see that you have zeal, they will want to be around you just to find out what's going on. I remember a motivational speaker talking about the difference between a live volcano and a dead fish. People are attracted to watch a live volcano but no one is attracted to watch a dead fish, because there's no energy. He went on to say, "Some of you are building your businesses the same way. Some of you are fired up and enthusiastic, but some of you have about the same amount of energy as a dead fish, and you wonder why your business isn't growing! You need to be like a live volcano if you want results, because if you're not excited about it, why should anybody else be?"

Most people have varying amounts of zeal, some more than others, but sadly, some people are living without it completely. Some people are in a rut and it's the same old routine day in day out, week in week out, year after year. The highlight of their day is often coming home from work and watching TV. Some people don't even have any goals and are simply living their lives pay cheque to pay cheque, living for the weekend. A typical saying is, "Thank goodness it's Friday!"

What a sad way to live life! God wants you to enjoy every day, not just the weekend. Then they dread Sunday evenings because Monday morning is just around the corner. They often live their lives in fear and worry. If you are living only for the weekends, realise that you are wishing away twenty days a month of your life. That's approximately two-thirds of your life that you are wishing down the drain! God never intended any of us to live our lives like that! God wants us to enjoy every day, and He also wants us to enjoy what we do. The Bible says, "This is the day the Lord has made; let us rejoice and be glad in it." (Psalm 118:24).

If you don't enjoy what you do, it simply means you're in the wrong line of work and haven't yet found what you're looking for. But it's out there, so don't get discouraged and don't give up. Keep looking and stay enthusiastic. Ask for God's help. Ask him to provide you with an opportunity. The Bible tells us that God wants to give us the desires of our heart (see Psalm 37:4). He also has a plan for every one of us, if we will allow Him to work in our lives. "For I know the plans I have for you," declares the Lord, "plans to prosper you and not to harm you, plans to give you hope and a future." (Jer 29:11) But we must be willing to do our part.

We've got to be willing to step out of our comfort zone and take advantage of opportunity. We can't passively sit back expecting great things to happen if we aren't willing to do anything to help ourselves.

When you find your true calling in life, you will be operating with zeal every day. Your perspective will change from dreading Monday morning to looking forward to it as much as any other day of the week. That's how life should be lived! Instead of watching the clock all the time and living from tea break to tea break, time will fly and there won't be enough hours in the day. When you enjoy what you do, your whole perspective changes and your enthusiasm spills over into other areas of your life. That's when you're operating with zeal! When you have dreams and goals, you don't just get fired up about your dreams and goals; you get fired up about the whole of life. Life takes on a whole new meaning because you're going somewhere!

Maybe you don't like working for a boss, and the solution is to work for yourself. I know because I've been there! Years ago when I left school I didn't know what I wanted to do, so I ended up taking all kinds of jobs that I wasn't really interested in. I lived for the weekends because I hated my job, but I needed to go because I needed the pay cheque. Can you relate? I lacked zeal big time! In fact, it wasn't even part of my vocabulary back then. It wasn't that I was lazy or didn't like working; I just didn't like working for someone else, but I could see no way out of it.

But gradually, over a period of time, opportunities began to open up for me. People who I least expected gave me ideas for starting my own business with little or no risk financially. Others asked me if I was interested in joining them in a business venture. Eventually I did end up working for myself.

At the time I wasn't a Christian I and didn't realise that God was working in my life. I simply put it down to "good luck" to have ended up working for myself. But looking back now, I realise it was the work of God, because He knew what was in my heart. He will do the same for you. Rest assured that He's working in your life, right at this very moment. I also realised something else; God is faithful, even when we're not. God is always faithful. Faithful to us and faithful to His word! He wants you to be happy!

So remember, if you're going through pain just now, God sees everything. He knows you're hurting. But He wants to give you better than that. But you need to trust Him and have faith in Him, because God responds to faith. And last but not least, you need to have patience, because His timing is often different from ours. He might be allowing you to go through it for a reason. Maybe He's preparing you for something great and needs to strengthen you first? Maybe He's allowing you to go through it so that one day you can write about it and inspire other people? Maybe the zeal you lack just now will come back to you a hundredfold later on. Who knows?

The Bible tells us that, even in the tough times, God is using adversity for our highest long-term good. "And we know that in all things God works for the good of those who love him." (Rom 8:28)

I think the school system ought to shoulder some of the blame here. I think it sadly lacks in this area. We are taught at school how to get a job, but it teaches absolutely nothing about being self employed or owning your own business. Is it any surprise that some people go to work every day, to a job they hate, with zero enthusiasm? I don't think so. Teachers might say, "What do you want to be when you leave school?" In other words, they expect you to come up with some kind of fancy job title or profession that puts you in the category of employee rather than business owner. Therefore, young people are being geared from a very early age to think along the lines of being an employee instead of expanding their minds and thinking outside the box. Don't get me wrong, I'm not saying the school system is totally to blame, because sometimes it's the fault of the individual if they lack enthusiasm. Often it can be sheer laziness or just a downright negative attitude. But either way, we need to find our true calling in life. I think the first question we should be asked at school is, "Do you want to work for yourself or someone else?" And only then should it be narrowed down into specific categories or professions.

What has all this got to do with zeal? Quite a lot, actually, because there are a hell of a lot of people who go to work every day who don't have an ounce of zeal. Therefore, it's imperative that we find our true calling in life if we want to be happy, and to have this positive energy radiating from us in our daily lives. Zeal is the opposite of depression. Often, the reason many people don't have zeal in their lives is because they don't have any goals. They don't have anything to aim for, and as a result, they lack motivation. Therefore, they lack energy. They're maybe working hard every day and giving their employer one hundred percent, but if they don't like what they do and they don't have any goals, life can seem empty and sometimes meaningless.

Life without dreams or goals is drudgery, which is not what God intends for us. God wants us to live our lives with purpose and enthusiasm. He created us to achieve. When you discover what your dreams are, then you can start setting some goals to achieve them.

Once you do that, your life will take on a whole new meaning, because you'll be living life with a purpose. This is what I call the difference between living and merely existing. People who are living with purpose have far more energy, excitement, and enthusiasm than people who are merely existing. When you're living like this, you're also happier and your immune system is stronger because of your positive emotions. People who are living life with excitement and enthusiasm and have dreams and goals usually have less physical ailments than someone who is merely existing and has no goals. What makes the difference?

The difference, I believe, is twofold; firstly, the emotions, and secondly, focus.

Remember that positive emotions such as zeal and enthusiasm not only strengthen our immune system but also increase the strength in our physical bodies. This, in turn, helps us to fight off ailments and maladies that might normally have gotten the best of us had we been suffering from negative emotions. Studies on people watching extremely gruesome, bloody films on TV showed that their immune system was considerably weakened as a result of experiencing negative emotions. In this negative emotional state, it would have been virtually impossible for enthusiasm to exist. This would also have had a corresponding effect on their physical bodies.

Secondly, I believe that focus also plays a part in our physical wellbeing, because people with no dreams or goals have more time on their hands and are more liable to focus on negative things. Therefore, they also have more time to worry. Unlike people who are in the pursuit of their dreams and goals, they have far more time to focus on things such as TV, newspapers, the latest gossip, etc. They also have more time to focus on themselves, which is not a good thing if you want to be happy and successful. Self focus, especially if you're feeling down, tends to lead to other negative emotions such as self-pity, worry, anxiety, and sometimes fear, which creates a downward spiral.

But people in pursuit of their dreams don't have time for any of that. They're simply too busy and their focus is different because they're focusing on positive things instead. A different focus creates a different emotional response. When we focus on negative things it creates negative emotions, but when we focus on positive things it creates positive emotions.

A lack of dreams or goals also destroys the positive emotion of hope. People without dreams or goals are far more likely to suffer from negative emotions than anyone else. They might be jealous of other people's achievements, they might lack hope for the future, they might worry about their finances, and they might possibly suffer from fear and anxiety as a result of watching the news on TV. They might even be angry as a result of where they are in life. But think how much better you feel when you focus on your dreams! You have excitement; you have energy and enthusiasm. It also gives you hope. You have a strong desire to achieve something and to help other people. You might even have faith that you'll get there! That's a whole lot better than sitting around at home watching TV and going nowhere.

As you can see, having dreams and goals and having a purpose profoundly affects every area of your life. That's why people with dreams or goals are less likely to suffer from depression. Have you ever noticed that people who are in the pursuit of something worthwhile are also happier? They're less likely to get agitated over little things and are more likely to rise above it than other people. Why? Because not only do they have zeal, but they are too focused on the big picture to let the small stuff bother them. "So what if someone cut you off in traffic, you're going to be financially independent!" is a typical winning attitude.

ALL NEGATIVE EMOTIONS DESTROY ZEAL

Zeal, like any positive emotion, can be instantly destroyed by the presence of negative emotions. Therefore, we need to recognise and stop any kind of behavior or actions that cause negative emotions. Negative emotions such as anger, worry, anxiety, jealousy, lust, hatred, bitterness, greed, fear, and rage all destroy our enthusiasm and will cause us to fail, unless we take control. If you want to be fired up and enthusiastic all the time, then you need to constantly be aware of your attitude and the words you speak, because everything you say will have either a positive or negative emotional response, and you will feel either better or worse for having said those words. Therefore you need to avoid any kind of pessimistic talk. What does it do to your enthusiasm if you moan and complain about the weather? It kills it! So why do it? We need to stop criticising people and putting them down, and we need to stop putting ourselves down. You need to speak positively about yourself and other people. Your subconscious doesn't care "who" you were talking about; it only cares about the emotions involved. Was it negative, putdown comments, or was it uplifting and positive? You also need to speak about winning instead of losing. All of this will help to keep you motivated and enthusiastic. Then you will be operating with zeal and headed towards your dreams.

ZEAL IS A CHOICE

Zeal is not something that happens to us as matter of chance. It is not a piece of luck if we waken up in the morning and feel enthusiastic. It is chosen. Everyone has the potential to be enthusiastic, but they need to make the choice. What you focus on determines your emotional state. Do you focus on positive or negative things? It has often been said that people are about as happy as they make up their minds to be. It's also a psychological principle that motion creates emotion. If you don't feel excited, act excited and you will start to feel excited. Just to prove a point, imagine someone sitting at home with their feet up, watching TV. They're bored! Lacking enthusiasm. They can't be bothered doing anything. Someone says to them, "Do you fancy going out for a walk?" They say "No, I can't be bothered, and it looks cold outside" Suddenly as they're watching TV, they see their lottery numbers coming up. They've won! So they jump up in the air, shouting and yelling. They run around the house telling everyone. They phone their best friend and say, "I'll be right over!"

Full of enthusiasm, they run half a mile along the road without a jacket and tell them the "good news." Now, where did that enthusiasm and energy come from? The answer is that it was within them all the time. The only difference was that before they heard the "good news," it was only potential energy. This means that it could either be tapped into or be left dormant. But because they had a strong enough reason, they chose to tap into it. We all have a reserve tank of zeal and enthusiasm just waiting to be tapped into. Some people utilise it and some don't.

Zeal first begins in the mind before we see any outward evidence in the body. Don't wait until something exciting happens before you get enthusiastic, because you might have a long wait. Act enthusiastic now, even if you don't feel like it, and you will become enthusiastic. Enthusiasm also has a lot to do with what you tell yourself. If you say that you hate Monday mornings, you will hate Monday mornings and you will kill any enthusiasm that you might've had. But if you tell yourself (especially out loud) that you love Monday mornings, you will feel much happier about Monday mornings because your attitude will be positive and you will program your subconscious mind to look for ways to make it a reality. Such little words can make such a big difference! Your subconscious will do whatever you say. Remember that your subconscious mind is your obedient servant, standing by, just waiting for your commands. Almost like a waiter standing by your table waiting to take your orders. The waiter won't say, "Now I don't think you should have that. There are a lot of calories in it." He will simply say, "Yes, Sir," even if it's bad for you. In the same way, your subconscious doesn't care if you are happy or unhappy, have negative emotions or positive emotions; it doesn't care if you are excited or depressed, it simply says,

"Yes Sir!"

Unlike our conscious mind, the subconscious cannot make decisions and has no reasoning of its own. Therefore, it cannot and does not argue back. A bit like a robot. Yet, the irony is that it's the subconscious which is the far more powerful of the two. Your subconscious not only creates your emotions, but it also determines what you attract, good or bad! Get your emotions right, and you will attract the right things!

Someone once said that nothing great was ever accomplished without enthusiasm, and it is true. But to stay enthusiastic we must work at it on a daily basis and control what goes into our minds. As far as possible we must only allow positive into our minds. Not too long ago I heard someone talking about a positive thinking book they had read. They said "It was a great book, but once you finish it, your enthusiasm quickly fades." I realised what they were saying was true, but what they failed to realise was that motivation is not permanent. No matter how good the book is, you need to keep reading constantly if you are to stay enthusiastic, or it will fade. It's like keeping physically fit. Even if you are fit as a fiddle just now, you won't stay that way if you choose to stop exercising.

Therefore, if you want to stay positive and enthusiastic, you need to read a little bit every day. Even five pages a day will do it, but it has to be every day. You need to make it as regular as bathing, so that not a day goes by without reading. It is my prayer that if you get nothing else from this book, you will commit to reading from a positive thinking book for at least fifteen minutes every day. Fifteen minutes out of twenty-four hours isn't much if it's going to change your life! Why not go for it? Why not commit to fifteen minutes a day and make it part of your life? What have you got to lose? Absolutely nothing! And what have you got to gain? Absolutely everything! It might be the best thing you ever did! I know that is certainly true for me. Apart from God Almighty, it's been the books I've read that have changed my life. They will do the same for you if, and only if, you never miss a day. That is non-negotiable. You can do it!

God Bless you!

About The Author

A ndy Holligan is an independent business owner in his native Scotland, Great Britain. He became involved in multi level marketing in 1995, which he worked part-time. The sales and training system changed his life- way beyond his expectations and he became a Christian in 1999.

What Holligan has written about in his books is based not on 'classroom theory', but on his own personal experience over a period of years. His hope is that other people might avoid the pitfalls he fell into and at the same time, benefit from what he has experienced. Please visit his website at:

www.solutionstoyourlife.com

Other titles by the same author:

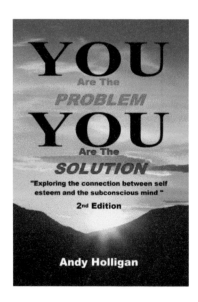

ISBN 978-1-911090-85-4

BV - #0017 - 190620 - C0 - 229/152/14 - PB - 9781911090854